Through Thick and Thin

Journeying through grief with God

Kathryn Cole

**Kingdom
Publishers**

A catalogue record for this book is available from the British Library.

All Scripture Quotations have been taken from the New International
Version of the Bible

ISBN: 978-1-911697-85-5

1st Edition 2023 by Kingdom Publishers, London, UK.

You can purchase copies of this book from any leading bookstore or
email **contact@kingdompublishers.co.uk**

Dedication

To all those who supported me through this time.

Contents

Foreword

Why do bad things happen to good people?

This is a question most of us ask when tragedy strikes. When it happens to people we know, our human, empathetic response kicks in and we immediately offer comfort and support. Cards, flowers, with offers of practical help surround and sometimes overwhelm those caught in the middle of the crisis.

Then there comes an inevitable lull in the attention as life moves on and we assume it's doing the same for our friends struggling with loss. Many who have walked this path speak about it being the hardest part of their heart-rending journey. It has been said, *"Grief tears a hole in the fabric of life that we spend the rest of our days trying to mend."*

Kathy Cole has written an honest account of her journey of repair following the unexpected death of her son, Rick, at the age of just twenty four. Rick was a few days short of his first wedding anniversary to Helen, and they stood at the brink of a lifetime of service for God.

Rick's death was an inexplicable and devastating loss.

Kathy and her husband, David, are passionate walkers and this provides a creative analogy to describe how she sought to process all that transpired following Rick's death.

When I first read the manuscript it was not intended for publication but, as Rick was a good friend and former student, Kathy wanted to share it with me as part of her grieving process. I found it profoundly moving and could see how her account might provide comfort and hope for others walking their personal paths of loss.

It is not a book with easy answers but it does point to the One who walks alongside and bears our griefs and our sorrows.

Ian Coffey
Moorlands College – Summer 2023

Introduction

My son, Rick, wrote a New Year message in the Church magazine for January 2015. He wrote about people in the bible who had been faithful, who listened to God, and who followed him through thick and thin. He invited the church to join him that year in listening to God, to see where he was going to take them. Rick was only to be with them for the first month of that year. In the March magazine the minister, in writing about Rick, quoted some of what he had written. She then went on to say of him, 'He was faithful, and he "listened to God and followed him through thick and thin." He would still say those words to us – listen to God.... see where God is going to take us...'

On 8th March 2015, I wrote in my journal, '31 January Rick died. My precious son was taken from me.' The death of your child is certainly a time when you discover how willing you are to follow God through thick and thin. This was made even harder by the continual battering of other things that life was throwing at us at that time. How can you remain faithful when you are drowning in a sea of questions, and nothing makes sense anymore? How can you find God when you are devastated, overwhelmed by pain and grief, exhausted, and often close to despair? How can you follow God when you cannot face people or life, and when you reach a point of total brokenness?

This was a journey through thick and thin that I had not imagined I would have to make, and most certainly one I had never wanted to have to face. It seemed unbearable, and I wasn't at all sure I could survive it. The shock of finding my life suddenly changed in this way, with no prior warning at all, was overwhelming. It was a very dark place that I found myself in, torn apart by loss. It was a journey there was no escape from, but I had choices along the way as to how I responded to the situation itself, and to God.

I have likened this journey to a walk through thick and thin which my husband, David, and I did in Northumberland. It was a lovely sunny August day, and we set off to do a walk from a book of guided walks. It was apparently 6 km and would take us 2 hours. We allowed extra time, so that we would not have to rush, and did not take our lunch as we would be back in plenty of time. This meant that we were not prepared for what happened next. The first part of the walk was on a well-defined path, with a few ups and downs, and the occasional boggy bit to negotiate, but fairly easy walking and enjoyable.

Then suddenly everything changed. The route took us off the path across an area of access land. We were ploughing through heather and going uphill over boggy ground. It was a relief to reach the next path, but after only a very short distance it disappeared. We were again wandering across boggy, uneven ground, making lots of detours as we went backwards and forwards trying to pick our way through. Occasionally we came across a short boardwalk, and we were very grateful for these respites from the exhausting walking.

Eventually, we came to a path taking us out of the bog. The trouble was it was a very narrow path up the side of a hill, with a steep drop to our right. At the top of the hill, we came to the remains of a forest area, where we had to negotiate tree stumps, felled trees, and water-logged ground. We could see the hill in the distance that we were heading towards, but I found that every time I looked at the hill we were no closer than the last time I had looked! To add to the difficulty I turned my ankle stepping off a boardwalk, but fortunately, the pain quickly subsided and I was able to carry on.

At this point, we met some people coming the other way. They told us it was not far to a track that would take us to the foot of the hill. It turned out their idea of not far was not the same as mine! We emerged from the forest area into more bog, and if anything this was the worst yet. It was at this point I gave up, and I sat down on a log, convinced I couldn't take another step. Giving up in the middle of nowhere, however, was not really an option. I had to find a way to continue.

I dragged myself on until at last, we reached the track, easily walking on firm ground at last. The trouble was the path then went up a steep hill! Having survived the difficult climb, we then had to negotiate a series of steep descents and ascents along the ridge. Coming to the top of each hill we hoped to see the car, but we kept being disappointed. Eventually, the car came into sight; the only trouble was it was just a dot in the distance. There was also a steep descent to be tackled to reach it, but five hours after leaving the car we made it back again. It was then, after removing my walking boots, that the result of the injury to my ankle gradually became more apparent.

We could not believe that a 6 km (3.7 miles) walk had taken us so long. We felt better when we measured it on the map and discovered that it was actually 6 miles, not 6 km! It was the toughest 6 miles we had ever walked, and not surprising that it had taken five hours. Others would have done it more quickly, others more slowly. It took as long as it took and could not be hurried. There are definite parallels between this walk and my journey following Rick's death. The terrain, the difficulties, the thoughts, and the feelings experienced on the walk all reflect different aspects of that journey.

I have kept a journal from that entry on the 8th of March 2015 to the present day. Sometimes I wrote daily, and at other times weekly, or longer. I used it to record things that were happening, my feelings, and my reactions, as a way of processing all that was going on through a truly bewildering time. I also recorded those things I felt God was showing me, the process of trying to find answers, and the highs and lows in my faith through that time. Often, I struggled to get my thoughts together, at other times the pen would not keep up with the words racing through my mind. The walk in Northumberland and my journal are the starting points for writing about my journey of following God through thick and thin.

Chapter 1 - My life experience

Walking had always been an enjoyable part of my life. I remember the thrill of getting my first pair of proper walking boots. We had several family holidays in Scotland, Wales, and the Lake District that included a lot of hill walking, and I loved it. Before we were married, David came on holiday with us and was subjected to days of walking, which to my relief he enjoyed. This has been an important part of our lives ever since. A couple of years after we were married, we went to Switzerland. We knew we were going to do a lot of strenuous walking, so we prepared by doing long walks in the Peak District, including Kinder Scout. The scenery and the wildflowers in Switzerland were amazing, and walking was the best way of experiencing it all. We walked up more than one mountain to places that were above the snow line in June. We had learnt to start off at a gradual pace, and we often saw that those who had overtaken us at the beginning failed to make it all the way. We do not walk as far, or as high these days, but we are still capable of 6-8 miles in the Peak District. So we were not inexperienced walkers, but the walk in Northumberland caught us out!

By my late fifties, I had experienced some of what life can throw at you, both good and bad. But nothing I had experienced up to that point had prepared me for the devastation of losing my child. Nothing can do that.

My life began in Walthamstow in 1956. It always feels strange to me, when I fill in a form, to have to put my place of birth as Walthamstow. I consider myself to be from Sussex, and that is where I grew up from the age of two. Tracing my family tree, I discovered that both sides of the family had lived in Sussex going back for generations. I don't remember anything about Walthamstow, and I feel no connection with it. My roots are in Sussex, I just wasn't born there. After my parents were married, my Dad's first job was as a history teacher at a school in Walthamstow. They weren't there for long, but I was born during that time and so officially it is where I am from.

Sussex was a lovely county to be brought up in. Sunday afternoons were always a time set aside for a family walk. We explored the Downs, the woods, the villages, the commons, and the National Trust gardens. It was lovely driving around Sussex too, with its leafy lanes and banks of wildflowers. I loved the colours and crunching through the fallen leaves in autumn. In the spring there were bluebells in the woods and cowslips on the Downs. We could hear the cuckoo, in the nearby woods, from our house, and on our walks on the Downs, we enjoyed the song of the skylarks. I would lie on my back, searching a clear blue sky for the tiny dot that was making the lovely sound so high above me.

We also made frequent trips to Newhaven to visit our grandparents. This sometimes included a walk along the breakwater, which went out to the lighthouse. I used to love running in and out of the arches, but the smell of rotting fish wasn't so pleasant. You could walk along the top of the arches, but I only attempted this once. The movement of the sea on both sides made me feel quite dizzy, and it was only a narrow walkway. We also spent time at Sandy Corner, which as its name suggests was a corner of sand between the breakwater and the front. It was fun to be in the sea when the ferry came into the harbour, as the wash created large waves. It was also fun to watch the people who didn't know about the wash, and were sitting too close to the water's edge!

My sister was born when I was three. We could be good friends but we did argue rather a lot. When I was eight, I enjoyed the addition of a baby brother to the family. I remember long, hot summers playing together in the garden, but that is probably not quite how it was. My memory of winter is that there was plenty of snow, which was fun at first, but then became slippery and hung around for too long. It was a time to sit in front of the fire with a book. We didn't have a television until I was older, but why did I need one when I had books? I escaped into the world of Narnia, the totally unrealistic lives of children like the Famous Five and girls at boarding school. I cried over Black Beauty and Heidi. I constantly had my nose in a book.

There was plenty to enjoy in my childhood. I didn't, however, always find things easy. I was painfully shy, which meant that school caused a certain amount of anxiety for me. My school reports always mentioned that I was too quiet in class. Academically I was fairly average. As an avid reader, English was no problem for me. Maths, however, was a different story and this was constantly pointed out in my school reports. One teacher expressed his concern about my consistently poor arithmetic results. He wrote, 'calculations of any kind seem to be of no interest to her.' It wasn't so much a lack of interest as a total lack of ability. Once we got to our final year, we had to sit the 11+ to determine which school we would go to next. My parents were told I was borderline. They decided that I would probably do better at the top of a Secondary school, rather than the bottom of a Grammar school, so I wasn't given extra tuition to get me through. I duly failed the 11+, which was fine by me as I wasn't too keen on going to the school where my Dad taught!

I went to a good Secondary school, where academic achievement was encouraged as well as providing more practical subjects. I had a lovely group of friends but was often in a state of anxiety over certain lessons. My school reports here describe me as hardworking and making good progress, but again I was too quiet in class and needed to have more confidence in my ability. Maths was not such a problem now, but I didn't find it easy. Other subjects I struggled with included Physics, Chemistry, and French. My school reports don't seem to reflect this though, so I must have reached a reasonable standard without really knowing what I was doing! My parents had been correct; I would have struggled with the pressure of Grammar school.

I managed to do sufficiently well at O-level to go on to the sixth form, at the Grammar school, to do A-levels. There was only a handful of us who did that, but we soon made friends with those who'd come from another Secondary school. I very quickly discovered that some of my new friends were Christians. I had chosen to do RE as one of my A-levels, simply because I wanted to do a subject that I hadn't done at O-level. For some reason, I also thought that it would be an easy option, but that quickly proved not to be the case. Both the RE teachers were Christians. I was about to have my eyes opened to something, which in spite of my church background had so far passed me by.

As a family, we had always gone to church, and I had been through the Sunday school. By this point, I was actually teaching the 4-5 year olds, but I wasn't sure whether I believed in God, and I certainly didn't understand what it meant to be a Christian. If God did exist then he was a distant, scary figure. One of my friends at Secondary school had a deep faith, and I rather envied her, but overall I preferred not to think about it. My new friends in the sixth form went to a church youth group and were constantly inviting me to things, but I wasn't at all sure about going. This continued until, in a General Studies lesson, we were asked to answer the question, 'what is your purpose in life?' This totally floored me as I realised that I hadn't got a purpose in life that really mattered. I started to listen more to what my friends were sharing with me, and to what I was hearing in RE, and I asked more questions. Eventually, I was persuaded to go to a meeting, where someone, who I sensed had a similar personality to me, shared what her faith meant to her. In the car, on the way home, I suddenly became totally convinced that God existed. There was no more doubt; I knew that I needed to do something about it. I had been given a booklet called Journey into Life, which explained in simple terms what it meant to be a Christian, and how to take the first step. It was as though what people had been telling me became clear and it all made sense. That night I asked for God's forgiveness and gave my life to him.

The two years in the sixth form, although I still struggled with shyness and lack of confidence, were the least anxious of my school life and the ones I enjoyed the most. My school reports still nagged me to contribute more in class, but a comment from my form tutor helped me to feel more acceptable as I was. He wrote, 'We have room for hard workers with gentle natures.' It was the first time a teacher had said anything positive about my personality. I was going to the church youth group on Saturday and Sunday evenings and I was working in the Co-op at weekends, so I'm not sure how I managed to fit in school work. I must have done though because I ended up with good grades at A-level. I somehow managed to find the confidence to get a place on the Biblical Studies course at Sheffield University. Again I made some good friends and enjoyed my three years as a student. The Biblical Studies department was fairly small and friendly, and I felt comfortable, but still had the usual anxieties. Why ever did I choose a course that involved learning two languages? I struggled with Greek and Hebrew and hated the lectures, which involved participation. The rest of the course was a challenge but was, on the whole, enjoyable.

Everyone seemed so much more confident than I was, and I felt this especially at the Christian Union. At the end of my second year, with a bit of a push, I took on organising the catering. I discovered being behind a counter serving tea and coffee was a more comfortable place than trying to mingle! I moved out of a hall of residence in the third year into a house with three friends. We prayed that we would be able to use the house in some way for God. I didn't for one minute think that would be through me, but I had reckoned without the CU Rep. She visited the Christian Unions in the north, to support, encourage, and help with organisation, and she was a formidable character. If she decided you were the right person for a job then you did it, it wasn't up for discussion! She decided I was the right person to lead a bible study group for those in the CU in digs close to our house, so I did it. It was certainly out of my comfort zone. However, I did feel it was right, as did the others in the house, and I discovered that when God asks you to do something for him then he gives you the strength to do it. It helped that at the end of the second year I had started going out with David and in this, as in many other things over the years, I had his support.

I graduated without any clear idea of what was to happen next. I couldn't get a grant to do the post-graduate secretarial course in Sheffield, which was what I really wanted to do. I got a place on a post A-level course in Sussex, but that really wasn't the same so I turned it down. David had gone home to Cheshire while he did his training to become a chartered accountant with a firm in Manchester. So I decided to stay in Sheffield and enrolled on a shorthand and typing evening class while I tried to find a job, without success. I found I was in the difficult position of being over-qualified with a degree for the jobs I was applying for, but I did not have the experience for jobs at a higher level. Neither did I have the necessary confidence in interviews. I got more and more depressed with the situation.

I decided to move to Cheshire to see if jobs were easier to come by that side of the Pennines. I was unsuccessful at first but eventually got a job in a pensions department. I hated it, dealing with figures all day was not my ideal job and there wasn't enough to do, so I was bored. The depression got worse and I eventually had to leave. I improved with the help of medication and having completed the evening course, by travelling back to Sheffield each week, I was able to get a secretarial job in a fabric printing company. Again there wasn't enough to do but it was only part-time at first, so I managed to cope with it. When someone left, I became full-time and took over her job as well as my own. It involved figures again, I'm not sure how I kept ending up with these jobs when Maths was really not my strong point!

Shortly after leaving university David and I had become engaged. He wanted to qualify before we got married, so we had a three-year engagement. Planning our wedding and buying our first house together was a welcome distraction from the boredom of work. We eventually got married in 1981 and had our honeymoon in Scotland, which of course included a lot of walking. Once back, on top of a demanding job with lots of travelling, David became the church treasurer, which involved meetings as well as keeping the books. Not a good start to a marriage as he had little time left over.

After three years our daughter, Anna, was born. It did not begin well as her birth, and the whole hospital experience, was definitely something I didn't want to repeat. As a lot of new Mums find, the first six weeks with Anna were not an easy time. I got more and more exhausted and ended up with post-natal depression. Once we had established more of a routine, and I gradually recovered, I began to enjoy being a Mum. I was in the fortunate position of being able to choose not to return to work, and I had found a role which I found fulfilling. I still struggled with the fact that David wasn't around much, and the pressure became worse when he became a manager. We both decided this wasn't the sort of lifestyle we wanted; we were aware that many marriages didn't survive it. He was offered a job by one of the firms he audited with less travelling and less pressure, so that was an improvement.

When Anna was in her second year at school, we went to a parents' evening and there was a display on a board which showed Anna was the only one in the class without siblings. I felt very guilty about this, but still not ready to face again what I'd been through. A while later I was having a cup of tea with a friend when the doorbell rang. I went to answer it to find a midwife on the doorstep asking to see my baby. She would not believe I hadn't got one; she obviously thought I was denying her access. Eventually, we managed to work out that she'd come to the wrong address! I told my friend and we were laughing about it; the next minute I was in floods of tears with a desperate longing for another baby and afraid I'd left it too late. My friend calmed me down, and when David came home I announced that I wanted to have another baby. He didn't have any objections, and so just before Anna's sixth birthday in 1990 Richard, or Rick as he later came to be known, was born. His very existence was due to a lost midwife!

Everything about his birth, the time in hospital, and managing him as a baby was so much easier this time. I was therefore able to enjoy him from the start. Everything was going fine until at six weeks I got pleurisy. This did not respond to antibiotics and I was told that it was a virus. I was also told I should be being looked after myself rather than looking after a baby; easier said than done! We managed for a bit, but the endless coughing and the pain, which made me wish I could stop breathing, gradually took its toll on me. The final straw was when Anna fell off the swing and broke her arm. It suddenly all became too much and I was back on the anti-depressants again. My Mum came to help out and that took the pressure out of the situation. The worst thing for me was not being able to do things for Rick, apart from feeding him, because of the pain. Eventually, I improved sufficiently to manage again.

Before having Rick I had become more involved in the church. I had been pushed into leading a home group, but it was when I was persuaded to help as a holiday club leader that I discovered what I really enjoyed doing, I loved working with children. I carried on each year with the holiday club, and I started teaching in Sunday school. When Anna went to Brownies, I was asked to cover for someone for one session and ended up as an Assistant Guider! As a result of the pleurisy my relationship with God changed. I didn't lose my faith and I carried on outwardly at church, but inside I was feeling it's all too difficult, and I was keeping God at a distance. This lasted for the next few years. During this time David moved to another church, but I stayed on because of the children's work.

In 1997 I was diagnosed with M.E. This debilitating illness took 10 years of my life. I had many symptoms, but the two main ones were weakness and brain fog. Sometimes it felt like too much effort just to lie in bed. Mostly I was able to get up but do very little. At other times, especially in the summer, I improved and was able to do more. I constantly had to be careful not to do too much, but how much was too much? It varied from day to day, and there was always a price to pay for getting it wrong. The brain fog made concentration, conversation, and processing very difficult, and at times impossible. I had to give up the children's work, and I had to watch my family doing most of the things I should have been doing at home. Life became a matter of survival and felt very narrow and restricted. I felt I was missing out on so much in my children's lives, and I was restricting the things we were able to do together as a family. The result of all this was that I felt very frustrated, guilty, depressed, anxious, and useless. M.E had a stigma attached to it as some doctors did not believe in its existence. This, coupled with some people's attitudes towards me, made me feel I was unacceptable and a failure. My self-esteem was very low and I was robbed of what little confidence I'd had. M.E. destroys you as a person.

I turned back to God during this time, but the brain fog made praying very difficult, and for several years I was rarely able to go to church. When I did go to church, I had to go with David as I couldn't manage to go on my own. This meant I was at a church where I didn't know anyone, and I was too exhausted to do anything to change this. I felt isolated from everything that was going on around me. I slowly became aware of the love and care, and I felt accepted, in spite of the M.E. I found that at times God gave me the strength to do things that shouldn't have been possible. One of these was when I was accepted as a writer of Sunday school material by Scripture Union. It felt like being given a wonderful gift and it was exciting to discover God could still use me. He gave me the strength, ideas, and concentration I needed, and I managed to meet every deadline. A change of editor, who wanted more commitment than I was able to give, meant I could no longer carry on. It was a huge loss to me and I felt useless again.

After seven years of struggle, I went through a very bad patch. I was in despair as I tried to accept that I might be like this for the rest of my life. I could see no point in it, and I felt God had abandoned me. One evening God gave me the strength to go to a healing service at church and to go forward for prayer. There was an immediate change physically, which continued over the next few days. There was, however, more that God wanted to show me. The next three years were a journey as God continued to heal me physically, but also emotionally and spiritually. As M.E. had periods of remission, it took me a while to realise that I had actually recovered. I had slowly come back to life.

I emerged from M.E. with a new-found confidence in God and that he could use me. It was very special to be able to go back to working with children again. I organised the summer holiday club for the next eight years, and led an Urban Saints group for 4-7 year olds. David became an Elder and I got involved in the organisation of other events, and even spoke at several evening services. I felt like a different person, and even though I was quite often out of my comfort zone I knew God would give me the strength.

It was during this time that we discovered that Anna was struggling with anorexia. She was working in a local nursery but living independently, and I hadn't realised how serious her weight loss was. It was so hard watching her getting thinner and weaker until she was ill enough to go into hospital. She put on weight and recovered enough to go and work as a Nanny in Reading. From there she went to work with a family in New Zealand! It was painful saying goodbye, knowing that she wasn't well and she was going to be on the other side of the world.

It turned out New Zealand was good for her, and she renewed her visa and was there for over two years. This all changed when her visa eventually ran out and she had to leave the life that she had built up for herself there. Out of the blue, we had a phone call from a psychiatrist in New Zealand, and we began to learn that Anna's mental health illness was more complex than we had realised, and that she had a multiple diagnosis. We discovered that an injury had resulted in her being prescribed codeine to which she had become addicted. It alleviated some of her symptoms as did self-harming. They didn't want her to fly back by herself, so David went out for a three-week holiday and to bring her home.

We then discovered the lack of support from an overburdened mental health service. Anna gave up waiting to see a psychiatrist and got a job in Australia. Another painful parting, but with the hope that it would help her as being in New Zealand had done. It didn't, and that was a very stressful year. When she returned, I started to try to get her help, but each trip to A&E resulted in another assessment and then nothing further. I totally understood the need for confidentiality but it meant I was working in the dark, I only knew what Anna chose to tell me. She eventually got to see a psychiatrist, but still nothing was being done to help her. I found a residential place and the psychiatrist agreed it was just what she needed, but then funding was an issue, so we were no further forward.

Anna had a loving, warm, caring, and generous personality with a lot to give. It was heart-breaking to see this disappear as a result of her illness, with only glimpses of who she really was. She became an unpredictable stranger who I couldn't read at all, and who I felt the need to tiptoe around in case I did or said anything to make things worse. She would appear cheerful at tea time then a couple of hours later I could be taking her to A&E. I didn't know how to support her. I felt helpless, I was struggling to cope, and I was living in fear of losing her. This was the position I was in on the 31st of January 2015.

Chapter 2 - Enjoying the walk

The walk in Northumberland started out with so much promise. The weather was good, and the views were stunning with heather in every direction as far as the eye could see. We took our time, stopping to do some bird watching and enjoying the beauty and peace. It was a special place. The path was wide and easy to follow. It was an undulating path and steep in places. There were a few boggy patches in the dips, but these weren't hard to negotiate. It had its harder parts, but overall it was reasonably easy walking, and there was so much to enjoy on the way.

This first part of the walk describes how it was having Rick in my life. It was enjoyable and special, and held so much promise for the future. We both had our ups and downs and our harder times, but my bond with Rick was always a positive and precious thing for me throughout. He did me good and I always felt privileged to have a son like him.

Once I recovered from pleurisy I enjoyed the early years with Rick. He was very affectionate with a great sense of humour and an infectious giggle, which had us laughing with him without knowing what we were laughing at! He was a very easy child apart from when he got over-tired, and then nobody could do anything right. We used to send Anna to sort him out and she usually managed it. There was one notable occasion when she didn't. We were nearing the end of a walk when Rick suddenly sat down on a rock and refused to move, or to be carried. He screamed at us if we went back to him and screamed if we walked away. Promises and threats made no difference! In the end, there was nothing for it, David had to ignore his screams, pick him up, and carry him to the car park. Anna and I hung back out of embarrassment. I wanted to tell people that he was a lovely little boy really! He was a good walker in his little red wellies, but that time we had pushed him too far.

Another time he would get very upset was when he had his hair cut. Fortunately, I was able to take him to a friend, so the screaming sessions took place in the privacy of her home. We had no idea why he reacted like this, but it was something which had to be done, so we both tried hard to distract him while she cut his hair as best she could with a moving target. Much to my relief, he grew out of both this and his reaction to being over-tired.

Although Rick was a good walker, he was quite a cautious child when it came to physical activities. We did, however, have lots of fun when I took him swimming. He could be mischievous, and his sense of fun and enjoyment in what he was doing made it hard to tell him off. He loved playing with cars and any sort of construction toys. We undertook many building projects together, which increased in difficulty as he got older. We enjoyed doing craft activities together, but he wasn't so keen on colouring. He also had a love of books and enjoyed being read to. Sadly this time together was reduced as he went to playgroup and then again as he reached school age.

Rick was ready to learn and soon settled into school life. His first school report describes him as, 'a very capable, friendly little boy who happily participates in all areas of the curriculum.' Throughout his time at primary school, he had the label 'an excellent all-rounder,' though towards the end it was becoming apparent that he wasn't quite so excellent at P.E. He was enthusiastic, hardworking, and often asked questions. Unlike his mother, he had an aptitude for Maths, he was confident, and he contributed to class and group discussions!

All was going well until he got to year 4 at the age of eight. He had a succession of viruses and then began to get worked up about going to school. Several times I had to pick him up from school at lunchtime because he was feeling sick. His recovery was instantaneous; he would skip along beside me on the way home and polish off his lunch when we got there! Life for Rick had become more of a struggle as he battled with feeling sick both before and during school, and before going to other activities. Various tests did not reveal anything and the doctor told me that he was doing it to himself. No further help was offered. We never discovered the root cause of his anxiety. We just tried to support and encourage him as best we could. It would be something he struggled with, to a greater or lesser degree, for the rest of his life.

As he was growing up Rick went through various phases including Power Rangers, Pokemon, Egyptians and hieroglyphics, dinosaurs, and stamp collecting. He loved reading and I enjoyed the Narnia books all over again with him. Harry Potter was a definite favourite. As they had been for me, books for Rick were a way to escape. He enjoyed playing computer games, but that was an interest I didn't share. Rick loved cooking from an early age, and he was determined to do it with as little interference from me as possible, messy but enjoyable!

Rick didn't find the move to secondary school easy. Especially hard was when, after only a few weeks, they went to Conway for a week of team-building exercises. He survived this, just, and then settled into the school. Academically he continued in the same way over all subjects. He enjoyed learning, but I think sometimes he was bored. He had a quick mind and grasped something the first time it was explained, and then he had to wait for others to catch up. He had the desire to achieve. Not being satisfied with his predicted grade at German GCSE he worked hard to improve it, even though it was a subject he did not particularly enjoy. He was very able, but he had to combine this with hard work to get higher grades at GCSE and A-level. He could have carried any subject on to A-level but opted for Maths, Further Maths, Physics and IT. I never thought a child of mine would be doing Further Maths! The trouble was he liked to talk to me about what he was doing and to explain things, but I was totally out of my depth.

Rick's Christian faith was an important part of his life. I was told by a church holiday club leader that he'd made a commitment at the age of five, but he didn't really remember that when he was older, and he made a further commitment as a teenager. He got baptised when he was sixteen, and he said that he had reached a point in his life where he had to decide whether to go all out for God, or not. Getting baptised was his answer to that question. He went all out for God in various ways. He gradually got more involved in church life. He was already on the technical team, which was right up his street. He also attended an Urban Saints group himself, and helped with the younger groups. He started a Christian Union in his school with a friend from church. He was totally open about his faith at school.

Music was important to Rick, both listening to it and playing. He learnt the keyboard and got as far as working for his Grade 5. However, he felt that this was taking the pleasure out of it, so he opted to just have lessons to improve without the pressure of exams. His teacher reckoned she'd watched Rick grow from a boy, who approached music in a very mathematical way, into a young man, who played with heart and soul. I think the change happened as he began to use his musical ability for God and started to play for worship. He formed a band at church called Inspiration. They led evening Praise and Worship services, and he took the opportunity to introduce newer songs to the church. He worked hard to get the band playing in the morning services too. He started to concentrate more on improving on the piano, and he played for the evening services.

Rick also learnt the flute and was teaching himself to play the guitar. He wanted to learn the drums too but we discouraged that! I spent a lot of time in Rick's room while he played the keyboard. As usual, he would explain things to me as I had little knowledge of music. He introduced me to new songs from Mission Praise and played songs we both liked, and we talked about both the words and the music. I loved those times, but I had no idea then what a problem they were going to cause me in the future.

Rick spoke at one of the praise and worship services when he was sixteen. I couldn't believe the content and delivery; he spoke with so much authority. This was the point at which I felt sure he should go into full-time ministry, but I kept that to myself. After this, he began to lead and speak at the evening service, and then the morning service. These were good opportunities for him, and convinced me even further of the direction he should take in the future.

He managed to leave school with four A's at A-level, despite having to cope with a collapsed lung in November of his final year. The question was what to do next. His IT teacher had told us, at a parent's evening, that Rick was good enough to work anywhere in the world with computers and earn a lot of money. I sat there thinking, "but that's not who Rick is." He decided to take a gap year, but we persuaded him to get a place to do computer science at university, so he had something to fall back on. He was offered a place at Manchester University and was keen on the course, but I think we all knew it wasn't where he would end up.

The opportunity arose for Rick to volunteer with the town's Christian Mission during his gap year. This involved working in the schools, in local churches, and with other church youth workers to put on events in the town. He was also beginning to recognise a call into full-time ministry, and he began to apply to Theological Colleges. He gained a place at Moorlands College, in Dorset, to study Applied Theology. After he'd accepted the place, I told him I'd thought he should go into ministry ever since I'd first heard him speak. It was meant to be a confirmation for him, but all he did was tell me off for not telling him sooner! I hadn't told him because I wanted him to come to this decision for himself, through God's calling and the guidance of others, rather than because his Mum thought he should!

At the end of his gap year, he didn't feel ready for college, so he became a Volunteer Youth Worker for a year. This was mainly in our church, but also other churches and he continued work in the schools. He completed a Youth Work course during this year at a local college. He also continued to be involved in all he'd done before in the church, he helped to organise and run different events, and lend a hand wherever it was needed. He had a real servant's heart. He helped me with the holiday clubs and the Urban Saints group, and I loved working with him. He was capable of leading them himself, but he never tried to take over from me, he just supported and encouraged. Those were two precious years with Rick I hadn't expected to have.

One of the things Rick and I enjoyed was going for walks together, which gave the opportunity for a good chat. He was very protective of me, because of the ME, and he used to give me his arm to hold. When he was about fifteen we were walking along like this when I saw two lads, about his age, approaching. I quickly removed my hand, but Rick took it, replaced it, and held it so I couldn't remove it again. He spoke to the two lads, and once they were out of earshot, I said I hadn't wanted him to be embarrassed. His reply was, 'I know, but I wasn't.' I don't think many teenage lads would have done that, but he was always mature for his age and wasn't afraid to be himself in front of his peers.

Many of our walks took place after dark. His powers of persuasion were such that, no matter how tired I was, he could get me out into the dark and cold. I always felt better for it and was glad that I had gone. Spending time with Rick somehow energised me. Not all of our chats took place on walks. Some were in the comfort of home, but they went on into the early hours of the morning. When he went to Moorlands, we would have one of these chats the night he came back home, even though he was tired, and we were just about to have several weeks together. They were very special times for me.

As well as getting me to go on walks, he used his powers of persuasion in other areas too. He could be so enthusiastic that I would get drawn in, sometimes against my better judgement. Whenever we went to a beach, paddling in the sea was compulsory as far as Rick was concerned. He could even get me paddling in the rain! At Minehead we walked into the sea then turned round and walked straight back out again. Even Rick was defeated by the cold that day. I would be persuaded to help with technical things at church. Actually, I was no help at all. He'd send me to get a 1-metre cable, which meant nothing to me. When I came back with the wrong one he never got annoyed, he would just take it off me and go to get the correct one. We had always played games as a family, but at Moorlands he was introduced to strategy board games, and he even persuaded me into playing them. I thought I'd be out of my depth, but Rick didn't and I found that he was right. I've been enjoying them ever since as long as they are not too complicated, or go on for too long.

Another thing he drew me into was sorting out his bedroom! Rick was extremely untidy. There often wasn't much carpet showing, and his bin had more rubbish around it than in it where he'd lobbed it across the room and missed. Every now and again he would have a major sort-out. This often involved moving the furniture around too, which included much discussion and measuring. He was always pleased with it and resolved to keep it tidy, but this didn't last more than a few days.

Rick had a lot of patience. I know that because I put it to the test learning to use the computer. He was a natural teacher. I once asked him whether, as he was so quick to grasp things, he didn't feel impatient when others were slow to understand what he was trying to teach them. He replied that he just saw it as a challenge to find another way to explain it, so that they could grasp it. In other situations, he could be quite impatient. Although he was mature for his age, at times he could be typical of his age. When he thought he could see a solution to a problem, or something that needed to be changed he just wanted to get on and do it. He could get frustrated when others were more cautious, or didn't see things his way.

His enjoyment of cooking as a child continued. As he grew in confidence, he started experimenting with recipes and began cooking meals. I was happy to keep this interest going, although he always managed to leave the kitchen looking as though a bomb had hit it.

Having watched The Great British Bake Off, he decided we were going to make bread. As Rick was always up for a challenge, we didn't start with a basic loaf but went straight for the eight strand plaited loaf! We were quite surprised and pleased with the result. He also became a keen photographer, which combined his creative side with his love of anything technical. Our building projects had moved on to flat pack furniture. Rick was always in too much of a hurry to read the instructions properly, so invariably we had to remove pieces because another piece should have gone in first. He also built computers and I was called on to 'help.' Explanations were again forthcoming, as he taught me about the different parts and how they worked, and I found it fascinating.

He taught me most of what I know about using a computer. He would explain what I had to do and also why I had to do it, which made it so much easier to understand the process. He also went slowly enough for me to make copious step-by-step notes. He was always very willing to come and sort me out when I had a problem on the computer, and he did it without making me feel stupid. Apart from sorting me out, and others who came to him for help on their computers, Rick enjoyed graphic design. He also spent time teaching himself computer programming and he enjoyed the challenge of getting a programme to work.

Although we had our difficult times, there was a lot of laughter in our house with Rick around. He had a dry sense of humour and was very quick thinking in his responses. His laugh, although deeper than his childish giggle, was still infectious. There was a great deal of good humoured banter. He quickly recognised when this had gone too far for me and I was feeling got at, and he would give me a big hug. He never lost the willingness to show affection even as a teenager. He was loving and lovable, and he was very sensitive, understanding, and caring. He was always there for people who were hurting, or needed help in any way. He was a great encourager, and he helped me to believe in myself and what I could achieve.

Rick enjoyed his time at Moorlands, but found it tough. He continued to struggle with anxiety and was often being pushed out of his comfort zone. There was always a lot going on; keeping up with the academic work, college life, and involvement in a placement church. He continued his love of music by playing in the band at college and also at church. He enjoyed the course and, unlike me, he enjoyed Greek and Hebrew. At least now, when he talked to me about his work, I could understand what he was talking about! He had various physical illnesses to cope with during those three years. He also struggled with depression after he proposed to his girlfriend from home, which led to the discovery that she had been seeing someone else at her university. However, he did form some strong friendships at college, including Helen. This developed into a deeper relationship and they got engaged in their final year. They both graduated with first-class honours degrees. In a sermon, at his placement church, he described the struggle he'd had to get to this point and then said, 'I'm stood up on the stage and I'm talking to you and the only way that that is possible is through my God and my Saviour. He has done so much in my life.'

Having decided that he wanted to stay in the area, he ended up with two part-time jobs. The trouble was both of them were more than part-time, and Rick wasn't good at saying no. However, he enjoyed them both even though there were never enough hours in the day and it was a bit of a balancing act. He continued his association with Moorlands by working in the PR department. He also worked as a Youth and Family Worker in a Baptist Church. Here he ran holiday clubs in most of the school holidays, a weekly group for young people, and was again involved in anything that was asked of him. This included things that were outside his comfort zone. Walking through the town centre with two others dressed as the three kings, with cuddly toy camels under their arms, giving out details of the churches' Christmas services was definitely not something he was comfortable doing!

Wedding preparations were in full swing. Both Rick and Helen proved to be good at organising, which included an attention to detail. They wanted to make it a special time for their guests, as well as for themselves. There were one or two crises along the way, but these were handled and overcome together. They got married on a very wet and windy day in February 2014. Outdoor photos were not an option. Apart from that it was as special as they had planned it to be, and they left for a honeymoon in Venice.

They were a lovely couple. In the summer we joined some of their friends helping them to move from their flat, which they had outgrown very quickly, to a house. I was struck by how well they managed this together, and how considerate they were towards each other. They sought and valued each other's opinions. I also had the privilege of going to help Rick as a leader at one of his holiday clubs. I enjoyed the role reversal and not being the one responsible. It was a pleasure to spend time with the two of them on my own; I felt I had gained a daughter and not lost a son.

When they came at Christmas Rick and I had one of our walks together. He was very supportive over the situation with Anna. He told me he had taken the first step of approaching the Regional Minister of the Southern Counties Baptist Association to discuss going forward for ministerial recognition. We talked about the ways this could be done, and doing his MA at the same time as the training. A shorter time scale than he'd had in mind before starting this process was being suggested, and he was concerned about how they would cope financially. He had so many plans for the future as well as becoming a pastor in a Baptist Church. These included a PhD, and maybe eventually becoming a lecturer in a Bible College.

Towards the end of January Rick caught a virus. He continued to get worse, so went to the doctor who gave him some antibiotics in case there was an infection present. I rang him later that day which was Thursday. The doctor had told him he would be better by Monday. I spoke mostly to Helen as he was coughing so much, but he wanted to ask about Anna, showing his concern for her and for me. He said he hadn't felt so ill for years. I was sympathetic, but I believed the doctor, and my focus was elsewhere on what I thought were more pressing needs. On Saturday this was proved to be terribly wrong.

Chapter 3 - Everything changed

Our walk changed direction, and everything about it changed. We were no longer seeing a path stretching out ahead of us. We were in the shadow of a wood, so it was colder and darker. The ground was uneven and water-logged. It was gently uphill and we were fighting our way through the heather. Each step was hard work and precarious as we went from tussock to tussock. It was really tough walking and I felt in constant danger of falling. All the pleasure of the walk had been snatched away.

This sudden change is what happened to us on the 31st of January 2015. It was 7.13 on Saturday morning when the phone rang. This was unusual enough for me to feel apprehensive as I answered. I became even more apprehensive when I discovered that the person calling was a close friend of Rick's. I struggled to take in what he said next. Rick had gone into cardiac arrest and was being taken into hospital. He only had a virus, he was going to be better by Monday, how could this be happening? I desperately wanted to be with him, but we were a five hour drive away. Part of me knew it was too late, but I could not accept it. I told David what was happening, he prayed then immediately went into action, going to tell Anna, and then starting to get ready to leave. I just kept thinking 'I can't lose him, I can't.' I collapsed on the bed and my whole body was tingling. My head was telling me I needed to get ready to go, but I felt totally unable to move.

Eventually I got myself going, but I felt as though I was wandering around in a daze, and not functioning at all in the way I needed to. Once we were ready, I rang Rick's friend to see what was happening. It was

Helen who answered the phone and gave me the news that I had been expecting, but dreading. We were both crying and saying sorry to each other. It was such devastating news and my heart was breaking for her. She wanted us to come and I said we would talk when we were both calmer.

I cannot find the words to adequately describe how I felt when I put the phone down. I know that for a short time I lost it totally. It was as though part of me was being ripped away and the pain was unbearable. I didn't want to believe it. When the numbness came it was such a relief.

The rest of the day passed in a haze of disbelief, numbness and total bewilderment. I kept saying to myself 'Rick is dead' in an attempt to make myself believe what had happened, to try to take it in. As I sat looking out of the window at the snow on the ground, I thought that in the future every time it snowed it would bring back this moment. I also remember thinking that I had the choice of whether to sink or swim, and I determined that I would swim. I did not, at that point, fully realise what I was asking of myself.

Anna was adamant that she would not come to Helen's with us, and we did not want to leave her on her own. I felt torn between her and Helen, but I knew that Helen's parents were on their way to be with her, and she had support from friends. I'm not sure that we were in a state to manage the journey at that point anyway. Two of the elders and their wives came and talked and prayed with us. Everything felt so unreal. They were understandably upset and in shock, and I began to realise that I was going to have to cope with other people's reactions as well as my own. This brought me to the problem of how I was to tell my mother. I did not want her to be on her own when she heard. I suggested that we contact her minister and ask him to go and tell her. The Elders found his number and made the phone call for us, and we were very grateful when he agreed to go. It helped me to know that she had been offered support by the minister even though, when she rang me later, I discovered that she had chosen to be on her own.

Sunday carried on in pretty much the same way. It was a shock, and painful all over again when I woke up and remembered what had happened. After that the feeling of unreality returned. Two friends came to see me in the afternoon and it was good to have people there who I was close to, but I didn't feel that much like talking. Their shock and disbelief somehow intensified my own. Monday was more of the same except that the cards started arriving. At first I couldn't face opening them. After a day or two, as they piled up, it seemed ungrateful not to open them. They always reduced me to tears, but at the same time I appreciated the support and all that they said about Rick. I also found that I couldn't go into rooms of the house where there were photos of Rick. In the end I asked David to go round and remove them all. I found it too painful to look at the photos. I didn't question that, but just accepted that was how it was. As I was to discover so many times, a way needed to be found to make it more manageable. There was no point in making things harder than they needed to be.

On Tuesday we went for a walk to get some fresh air and to do something 'normal'. Much to our surprise, a couple we knew crossed the road to say to us how sorry they had been to hear about Rick. Whilst appreciating the fact that they had done that, I was wondering how on earth they knew. How had word got round so quickly, and to people I would not expect to know? For someone who is naturally a private person, this was very hard, and it triggered the feeling that I no longer wanted to go out in our local area. However, there was one good thing about so many people knowing. It meant that we had a lot of people praying for us; over the next few weeks I certainly felt upheld by those prayers.

We eventually set off for Dorset on Wednesday to see Helen, our first of four trips there and back over six weeks. It was a relief to be going, it was hard being at a distance and feeling disconnected from what was happening. We lived near a school and we managed to leave as parents were dropping off their children, bad timing! I was standing outside waiting for David to negotiate getting the car off the drive between parked cars in a narrow road. As I watched I was wondering how many of the people walking past knew what had happened. One of these was someone we knew from church. She saw me standing there, and she didn't hesitate but came across to give me a hug. She said, 'You go and we will pray.' She had no idea how much that meant to me and how strengthened I felt by it. I was beginning to learn that so often it is the small things that really help. It was especially encouraging as I felt totally unable to pray myself. At that point it seemed to me that God was not part of this unreal world, where nothing made sense anymore.

Helen's parents had rented a house for us all to stay in; it really helped not to have to cope with going to Rick and Helen's house on that first visit. It was a strange time, thinking about things I never thought I would have to think about; a funeral and thanksgiving service for my son. Helen wanted a burial rather than a cremation. It was her choice and I was never going to argue with her, but I was totally taken aback by this. On the rare occasions when we'd talked about that sort of thing, Rick had been adamant that he wanted to be cremated. So I did question it, but he had told Helen that he didn't mind, as he wouldn't be here to know about it. I accepted that, but I found it very hard to come to terms with a burial, a place where he would be, even though I knew that really his body was an empty shell. The idea of there being a grave to visit was an issue for me, guilt if I didn't, but not sure if I would be able to face it.

We met with the undertaker who suggested that we visited the cemetery, and also a woodland burial site. We went to the cemetery first and I hated it. You see a cemetery with fresh eyes when you are thinking of burying someone you love there. For some it will be absolutely the right place, for us it wasn't. The woodland burial site was different. It was a natural, peaceful place with a lake, and was not used as a cut through from one road to another. All the plaques were the same, small and simple. Each grave had a tree planted on it and was left to grow over naturally. If he had to be buried, then this was where I wanted it to be. Fortunately when Helen went, she felt the same.

The difficulty we had was we could not fix a date for the funeral. The post mortem had not revealed anything wrong with Rick's heart, so it was sent to a specialist in London. We had no idea how long all of this was going to take. We decided that we couldn't wait indefinitely before having the thanksgiving service, so we went ahead with arrangements for that. It meant we were able to choose a Saturday, making it easier for people to attend. Helen asked us if we wanted to say anything at the service. David said no, and my response was going to be the same. Before I could get the word out, I had this strong conviction that I should. I knew from past experience that convictions like this were from God. My immediate reaction was, 'surely not!' Seeing my hesitation Helen said that she was going to speak, which encouraged me. I also remembered that previously, when God had asked me to do something, he had given me the strength to do it. So even though I was thinking, 'how on earth am I going to do this,' I found that I was agreeing to speak.

One of the things that helped me on that first visit was being with people who, whilst grieving with us, had a strong faith. The minister from Rick's church was one of these. When she said, 'God's perspective is not the same as ours,' I felt almost a physical change as though something had shifted back into place inside me. I realised that although I did not understand what had happened, God did, and he was with me in it. I became aware that the unreal world into which I had been plunged did not cut me off from God. My steps across the boggy, uneven ground became, ever so slightly, more confident.

We only stayed a few days on that first visit. Eight days after Rick's death, Helen had to face what would have been their first wedding anniversary. Rick had arranged a weekend away, which had to be cancelled. It was a very hard day as I thought back to their wedding day, which had held so much hope for their future together. Being back at home was hard too, I felt in limbo. More cards, more flowers. Really appreciated, but so many reminders of what had happened. I didn't want to see anybody. I couldn't cope with people whose lives were carrying on as normal, when mine was so unreal. I also had to start thinking about what I was going to say at the Thanksgiving service. I found it a stressful thing to do as I needed to get it right. I had lots of ideas, but it was hard to decide what to put in and what to leave out. I found concentrating and thinking straight almost impossible, so just forming a sentence was a challenge. I knew what I wanted to say at the end about how much Rick had meant to me, and the rest came gradually.

Our second visit was made possible because Moorlands let us use a cottage they let out to students, who were away on block placement. It meant we could have extra time with Helen, while Anna went to visit my mother. Although appreciated, it felt like another strange thing, as we were living there amongst other people's belongings. There was plenty of wildlife at the cottage, both inside and out! Turning the corner on the stairs, I came face to face with a little mouse, which I proceeded to have a conversation with, albeit a one-sided one. It very politely sat and listened to me! Everything felt so unreal that talking to a mouse on the stairs did not seem at all a peculiar thing to be doing! I was most put out when David caught it and put it out in the garden. I would have let it go back to where it came from. Now it was as confused and lost as I was.

This time we had to face the house. It was so hard seeing Rick's car parked outside and his things lying around inside. There were lots of photos of him too, which my eyes kept being drawn towards even though it was so painful to look at them. It was two days before I could force myself to go into the kitchen, which I had helped him to sort out when they moved in. As he did most of the cooking, it felt very much his, and was the place in the house where I missed him the most. That time I only made cups of tea, but on our next visit I cooked in it a couple of times. It was so hard and felt so wrong to be doing it myself, rather than helping him.

We spent a lot of time on paperwork, phone calls, visits to banks etc. It was good that we were able to help Helen with all this, but it absorbed David more than me. I felt a bit of a spare part with too much time to think. We were also arranging the thanksgiving service, and visiting the burial ground to arrange the funeral, even though we couldn't fix a date. I was so grateful that Helen let us be a part of all that. We went to a service at Rick's church, as I didn't want the Thanksgiving service to be the first time I went back there. We sat at the back and I found I did not want to sing. It had nothing to do with the words; I just physically felt I couldn't sing. I was coping until we got to Shine Jesus Shine and then I lost it. It brought memories flooding back of singing it at the service on the Sunday after the holiday club, and how the teenagers had responded to it. It was the first time I realised what a strong trigger, for memories and grief, certain songs were going to be.

The minister's sermon on the refiner's fire challenged me. In the same way that fire is used to refine and test precious metals, so our faith will be tested to the limit to prove if it is genuine and to strengthen it (Zech 13:9). God can use the difficult circumstances in our lives to do this. I realised that it was what I did from here that was important; how I let God use this, both in my own life and for others. I could not make sense of what had happened, but I didn't want Rick's death to be meaningless. I wanted God to bring good out of it in some way in people's lives. I did not know how this was going to happen, and I realised that I would probably never know what happened. All I could do was trust that God would use it.

We returned home for a few days to be with Anna. I found it increasingly hard to go back. It was so much easier to be down south with the people whose daily lives had been affected by Rick's death, and who were grieving with us. I also found that their faith and their strength rubbed off on me, and I felt stronger for being with them. I was aware, however, that this was only going to be a temporary support. I knew that people from the church at home were grieving too. I knew that they loved us and wanted to support us, but I felt set apart from them all by tragedy and I couldn't face meeting them. The only people I could cope with seeing were those who had been with us over the first few days.

I had to finish what I was going to say at the Thanksgiving service. I was really struggling with how to write about his school life when the thought 'look at his school reports' came into my head. School reports were something I was never sure what to do with once they had been read and commented on, so they just got stuck in a drawer. I certainly hadn't been expecting to use them for this purpose, but extracting comments from them made a lot of what I wanted to say fall into place. I felt encouraged that God had asked me to speak and he was giving me the words to say. The problem was that I couldn't read it without crying. The minister was to be my back up if I couldn't read it, but I knew that it had become important to me that I spoke about Rick myself, and I felt sure God would help me. I sent her a copy and her response really made me feel that I had got it right, and gave me more assurance that I could do it.

So back down south again, this time for the Thanksgiving service. We were still able to use the college's cottage, and it helped so much not having to organise accommodation. The day before the service we were having lunch at Helen's and chatting together. It seemed to me the most relaxed we had been since Rick's death. Then the coroner rang and all that changed. Helen put him on speaker phone and we heard a cold, dispassionate voice telling us that Rick had died from sudden adult death syndrome, and this might have implications for any siblings and we should contact our GP. The conversation ended abruptly and I was stunned. I had lost my son, and now I was being told I might lose my daughter too. Helen could see that I needed to know more, so she rang her GP who kindly rang back to talk to us. She said that it could be hereditary and we would all need to be screened. I would not have believed that the nightmare could get any worse, but it just had. Surely it was enough that we had lost our son, without having to go through tests, and all the anxiety involved in that process. Walking across the boggy ground had suddenly become that much harder, and the hill seemed steeper. Somehow, I had to process this sufficiently to be able to focus on the service the next day.

Amazingly God got me through that and strengthened me. I felt calm and was able to trust him for the service. Unfortunately there was a traffic accident, which delayed people getting to the church. We just got through before the traffic got too bad, but Helen was stuck in it making it very stressful for her. It was hard waiting at the church for people to arrive so that the service could start, but God kept me calm. It was a very emotional, but at the same time positive, service. I managed to speak without crying, just! It felt like a very positive thing to have been able to talk to so many people about Rick, and what he had meant to me. I cried all the way through what Helen said as I felt so much for her and all she had lost. It was so hard to believe what was actually happening, that we were having a thanksgiving service for my 24 year old son. It was a celebration of his life, but more than that it was a positive focus on what Jesus had done for us, and what that meant for Rick and for us now and in the future. I think Rick would have approved!

We went to Moorlands afterwards, and God strengthened me for that time too as I talked to people. We were so grateful to everyone for coming, some driving long distances to be there. I was very touched too by the effort that was put into it by both the church and the college. They had made it all as easy as they could for us and had taken on a lot of the arrangements. It was wonderful to be supported in this way, and along with the use of the cottage and the ongoing support for Helen, I felt that we had seen love in action in a very real way.

Back home again to be with Anna, and then back to Dorset again for the burial. The students were back, so this time we had to arrange accommodation. We had stayed in a cottage, near to the college, for a week's holiday in Rick's first year, and this was available. It helped to be in a place which was familiar, and was our own space for a few days. I was dreading the burial, but I felt remarkably calm in the morning. We went for a walk by the sea and everything felt so unreal. It became very real though when we got to the burial ground. We had decided to keep the service brief and we had none of our family or friends there, but once again we were supported by the minister and others from the college. As we walked to the graveside I had a moment where I just wanted to turn and run, but David had firm hold of my hand and he was pulling me forward. It was so awful seeing the coffin and I cried from that point on all the way through the service. It was all too real, yet so unreal. I don't remember much about that service, other than that I wanted it to end. Afterwards we went to a car park on the cliffs and sat looking out over the sea, which was very calming.

We had felt that we would need a bit of space and time before going home, so we had booked the next three days at the cottage. I tried to keep going, but when we went shopping the next morning everything caught up with me. I suddenly became totally exhausted, totally uninterested in buying food for the next few days, totally unable to make decisions or process in any way. I dragged myself round the shop feeling on the edge of collapse. I spent the rest of the day resting, and the next two days were a mixture of walking, sleeping and spending time with Helen. The Sunday was Mother's Day, very hard to cope with three days after burying your son. We went for a walk by the sea, which as always helped me. Overall the short break did me good, I felt more positive at the end of it, and more ready to face going home.

Chapter 4 - Through the bog

We eventually came to a path, which was our turning to the right, but the relief was short-lived. We were very quickly thrown back into a boggy area, with no discernible path, and uneven ground with heather and tall grasses to negotiate. There were posts marking the route, but they were so far apart we had to use binoculars to try and find the next one. Even if we did manage to locate the next post it was impossible to work out how to get there. We seemed to be aimlessly wandering to and fro as we tried to find the least boggy bit to walk on. We were constantly retracing our steps as we got to a point which was impassable. It seemed endless, and we were becoming concerned about how much further we still had to go.

The short stretch of path was like the closure I felt after the burial. We had done all we needed to do, and the feeling of being in limbo we'd had for the last six weeks was over. This respite did not last long, however, and very soon I was struggling with the bog again, and it was just as hard, and I was just as lost. How do you find your way through grief and how do you begin to come to terms with the loss? I could not begin to work out how to get through it. On top of the grief, we had all sorts of other things to deal with. The bog was one step at a time; my life was one day at a time, sometimes one hour, or even one minute at a time. It seemed like a long way to go with no end in sight. I was constantly making a little bit of progress then being knocked back to where I'd come from.

We were made aware of the first issue we had to deal with before we'd even got home! We were nearly back when we got a text from Anna telling us that she was in hospital. She had not wanted to come to the Thanksgiving service, or the burial. I respected that, but found it really hard to leave her behind. She had assured us that she would be all right, but, quite understandably, she wasn't. On top of her illness and the struggle she was having, she then had to deal with the shock and trauma of losing her brother to whom she had been very close. It was far too much, and the next day she was sectioned. Although it was a shock for all of us, it raised my hopes that something would be done for her. This proved not to be the case, and she was not in hospital for long.

When we arrived home, one of the first things David did was to clear away all the cards we had received. It seemed to me to be his way of saying that, as far as possible, life needed to return to normal. But what was normal? As far as I was concerned normal had totally disappeared. I did try to pick up some of the threads of my life over the next few weeks, but at a much slower rate than David did. There were ordinary day to day jobs that needed to be got through, which at least gave a bit of structure. I had been doing a Bible correspondence course, and I was approaching deadlines for some essays. I felt I wanted to carry on with it because Rick had encouraged me to do it. I also managed to return to leading the children's group, but I couldn't face church.

None of this dispelled the feeling of unreality, and the sense of being disconnected from everyone. On the 30th March I wrote in my journal, 'There is definitely a before and after feeling. Before 31st January seems such a long time ago but it is only 8 weeks. Although some things are continuing from one to the other, I feel very different and am in a totally different place. I feel as if I'm living on a different plane to everyone else.' Spring is my favourite time of year, but I found that, although I could recognise the beauty of it, everything seemed dulled. I love being beside water, but I was finding that even that had no effect on me. It was as if part of me was dead inside and I was unable to respond. It was a lonely place to be, feeling at a distance from everyone and everything. I didn't even feel that close to David as we tried to cope in different ways, and tried to protect each other by not sharing our feelings.

It was important to me to continue to support Helen, but it was hard to be doing it from a distance. We Skyped regularly and I was so pleased that she still wanted us to be a part of her life. I really didn't want to lose her too. The Skype calls were helpful as we encouraged and supported each other, but it was far better when we could be together. When we managed to fit in a visit it was lovely to be with her, but it was so hard to be in the house. I so longed for Rick to walk in and I still found the photos a problem. Hardest of all though was still cooking by myself in 'Rick's' kitchen.

Lack of motivation and tiredness are constant themes in my journal. I was dragging myself through each day, and everything I had to do was a struggle. Things I'd done for years, like cooking meals, suddenly seemed too complicated. I often found that I was totally unable to concentrate. Even simple decisions were beyond me. Just deciding what to put on in the morning could take a long time. I could not remain focussed on the task in hand. I also felt trapped because I didn't want to go out by myself. I was afraid of meeting people who knew about Rick, and who would be sympathetic, or someone who didn't know, and who might ask after him. When I was with other people, I struggled with conversations because of the feeling of unreality. As I felt so detached and isolated from normal life, I struggled to cope with it going on around me. I could no longer watch the news as I couldn't cope with the emotion I felt for people facing hard situations, or the awful things that go on in the world.

As time went on, I found that a pattern developed with several days where I was not able to function much at all. These were followed by slightly more positive days, where I had the energy and motivation to do a bit more. On the best of these days, I was able to attempt harder things that I hadn't been able to face, like going into town. The first time I attempted this I felt like a rabbit, constantly on the alert for danger, and ready to bolt down a hole should I see it approaching in the form of someone I knew! It was a relief to find I could do even small things that had been part of my life before, which I'd done without thinking twice about, only to find another day that they had become impossible again. Doing my course and the children's group would sometimes be a welcome distraction. At other times, they were a burden and a pressure I struggled to cope with. The bad days were often triggered by ongoing situations, which were draining me on top of the exhaustion caused by bereavement.

I had been finding it hard to cope with the lack of support for Anna before Rick died. This continued, and although everyone agreed she needed to go to a residential unit, nobody did anything about it. She is a strong person, and she tried to continue with the voluntary work she had been doing. It was hard for her though, and she continued to self-medicate, by taking codeine, and self-harming in order to cope. I found it increasingly hard living in the same house as someone behaving in this way, and constantly wondering when the next crisis would occur, I was so scared of losing her. I also felt useless as I didn't know how to support her, or help her. I felt I had nothing to give because of what I was going through, and I felt I was letting her down. I was in a constant state of anxiety as she spent many hours in her room, and I had no way of knowing if she was all right. It was a relief when, after a long period of silence, I could hear her moving around. I constantly felt on overload, and the pressure of this began to take its toll on me. I was often in despair, and felt I was very close to breaking point.

This all came to a head through August, and eventually she was admitted to hospital to go through withdrawal from the codeine. At the end of this she was sectioned, but at last we had a psychiatrist who decided something really needed to be done. He was trying to work out a treatment plan, which he thought should be residential. He wanted her to stay in hospital while they found a suitable place and got funding. I felt for her, but I was relieved that she was safe. Only she wasn't as safe as I thought. She turned out to be a bit of an escape artist, and she used these opportunities to get codeine or to self-harm. The result of this was that we had visits from the police, and we even had our house searched while we were away. I dreaded the phone ringing, in case it was the hospital informing us she was missing. Fortunately she would answer her phone when I rang her, but it would take a bit of persuading to get her to tell me where she was. After a while, she was allowed occasional leave from the hospital, but I could only cope with it being on the condition that one of us was with her all the time, which she wasn't happy about. I couldn't face her being on her own in her room. I'd stood back and given her space for over 18 months, but at that point I felt things had to be on my terms, for both our sakes, whilst supporting her and giving her what she needed as much as possible. It was good to have her with us, but it could be exhausting. This was an incredibly stressful situation, but at last a place was found and the funding approved.

Another thing that had to be dealt with was the screening process, to see whether the cause of Rick's death was hereditary. This was started by the GP with a referral to a cardiologist. He couldn't have been nicer, but my heart sank as he outlined the four tests we would need to have. We were told that they rarely find anything in families, it wasn't being used for research, and they can't do anything about it if they do find anything, other than suggest things to avoid. I wondered what the point was, but felt compelled to go along with it for the sake of Anna and the wider family. It all felt part of nothing making sense anymore.

The whole process took nearly a year from the point at which the coroner first told us that we needed to contact our GP. That was a long time, especially when you are feeling vulnerable, to have the possibility hanging over you that Sudden Adult Death Syndrome might affect other people you love, as it had Rick. The tests were spaced out through this time then we had to wait months for the results. I felt unable to move forward, and it seemed like a huge intrusion on the grieving process. Even though I knew they were being done for our benefit, my reaction was to resent the tests, and I felt angry that we were being put through them. Obviously they weren't compulsory, but it felt as if they were.

The first test was a heart monitor, which was more of an inconvenience than anything else. The exercise test was worse as I'd never been on a treadmill before, and apparently I was doing it all wrong. It didn't feel a natural way to walk to me, and I found it stressful being all wired up. When they increased the speed I couldn't adjust my stride and it felt out of control. I panicked and had to stop. Then it was David's turn and he was gone for a long time. He eventually came back, looking as white as a sheet, with a nurse who explained his blood pressure had dropped and he'd been dizzy. We had to go and get him something to eat, and wait quarter of an hour before we could leave. I felt shaken up by the whole experience, especially as it had made me think about what had happened to Rick, and I was struggling to control my feelings. Anna got off lightly as she only had to have these two tests and her scan was an ultra-sound.

The ajmaline test to see if we had Bruger's syndrome came next. Over a month before hand, we were sent information about it, and it didn't sound good. I felt very apprehensive about having it done. David asked if he had the test first, and was found to be positive, would there be any need for me to have the test. The answer was yes there would, because they wanted to be thorough. I appreciated that, but I was surprised, as the chances of one of us having Bruger's syndrome were not high, never mind both of us. A lot of other things were happening at this point, so I felt very low as I tried to cope with these, and the dread of the test. As so often happened, with people praying for me I felt peaceful on the day. It was thoroughly unpleasant being attached to a machine by so many wires, and then having ajmaline injected to see what would happen. Fortunately nothing did and we were both negative. It was good to have the result of a test straight away.

The final test was an MRI scan. Not a pleasant thought if you are not keen on small spaces. As they had found nothing so far I was hoping we wouldn't have to do it. That was not to be, it was unlikely they would find anything, but it needed to be done for completeness and thoroughness. At first I said I wouldn't have it done, I felt I'd been thorough enough! Gradually I changed my mind, as I couldn't live with the thought that I wouldn't have done everything I could. When I actually saw how small the scanner was I thought I couldn't possibly do it. However, God gave me the strength and peace to go through with it and I survived the 30 minutes, although I felt shaky afterwards. When we got home, instead of the quiet evening we had planned, we were bombarded with four more situations that had to be dealt with, by the end of which I felt totally drained. The battering really was relentless.

Three and a half months later David finally got his result. It was over for him, but not for me. After that length of time I didn't expect there to be anything wrong, but there was to be a sting in the tail. We left it a few days and then decided to chase my result, which led to a phone call from the consultant. It was a relief to find that there was nothing wrong that would affect anybody else, but a shock that I had something on my right lung. I needed to have a CT scan to see more clearly what it was. My MRI scan had somehow got lost in the system, and the consultant only saw it as a result of our phone call. At least this meant that the CT scan and the results happened quickly. Fortunately, it turned out to be scarring from when I'd had pleurisy. It took a while to recover from this scare, and the depths to which it had plunged me. It didn't help that the first anniversary of Rick's death was during this time.

To add to all this, from April, we were living next to a building site. Our house adjoined the bottom of the garden of the house on the corner of our road. The owners of this house built a bungalow in their garden, very close to our house. The noise and the invasion of privacy were both hard to cope with. Towards the end of the build, they discovered that they couldn't connect the sewage in the way that they had thought, and their cheapest option was to connect to ours. We really didn't need this extra hassle of sorting it out through solicitors, and it wasn't our problem, but we were 'persuaded' to co-operate. Unpleasant e-mails really upset me when I felt so fragile and vulnerable, and I found it very stressful, but David calmly sorted it out on his terms.

One evening, we had a machine operating outside on the trenches they had dug for pipes. It was very noisy, and from time to time it caused our house to shake. The next morning, I went to answer the phone and struggled to open the dining room door. When I eventually got in, it was to find books had been blocking the door, they were everywhere, and the shelves from the wall were on top of the desk. After I'd answered the phone, and been very short with the person trying to sell me something, I just lost it. I couldn't stop crying, it was one more thing to sort out, and it felt like the last straw. The shelves had been up for a good thirty years, so it was presumably caused by the vibrations. Once we cleared the books and the shelves, we found that the desk was broken. We managed to find a bookcase in a charity furniture shop and some friends, who happened to be there with a large car, offered to deliver it for us. David managed to mend the desk, and we lived with the mess it had made of the wall. So that particular problem was easier to sort out than we thought it was going to be.

In December I developed bursitis in my hip. It started with an ache in the afternoon. In the evening my mother rang to say she had broken her wrist. I started to look up train times to Sussex, but was in enough pain to wonder how I was going to manage the London underground. By the end of the evening, I could barely walk. There was no way I could manage the journey, and I wouldn't have been much use when I got there. My mother coped, but I felt bad not being able to help her. It improved, but I was restricted in what I could do for a while. We had been going to a line dancing class before Rick died, and it was something I had managed to get back to. I was finding it a welcome distraction and a challenge. I was unable to continue with this, and I really missed both the dancing and the people, who had welcomed us back in just the right way, without fuss.

I was coping with other losses in my life as well. The summer before Rick died, I had decided that I had done my last holiday club, and it was time to hand it over. It seemed strange not to be working on it through the summer as I had done for the last eight years, but I knew I couldn't have managed it. I had also decided I was going to give up the weekly children's group at the end of the school year. Having already made that decision, I didn't change it when Rick died. I found it hard to leave, but I was struggling to cope, and I didn't want the responsibility. Although it was a relief to finish, the only time I felt really alive was when I was with the children, so I missed it. I felt as though my life was gradually becoming emptier, and at the same time David was getting busier and busier. I began to feel rather alone and left behind.

This was compounded by the fact that I'd not been able to get back to church. Sunday became the hardest day of the week for me, as I debated each week whether I was ready to face church again. I felt that it would just be an endurance test, but at the same time it felt like a loss. My main concern was the music. There were so many songs that would have been reminders of Rick and the times we shared together in his room, as well as when he played in church. There were so many other memories associated with the things that he'd done in church too. I couldn't face so many people who knew about Rick either. As an Elder's wife I felt guilty about not going, but I'm sure the majority of people would have understood.

My friend's husband was the curate of a local Anglican church, and he suggested that I tried their mid-week communion, which was quiet with no hymns. It took me a while to feel strong enough to go, but I found it very friendly and welcoming, and just the sort of service I needed. I left straight after the end of the service as I didn't want to have to talk to anyone, but it felt like a safe place to be. I did eventually manage to return to my former church, but it felt more like a duty, and as I'd feared, I struggled with the music. I sat at the back, and would often have to walk out as strong memories were triggered, and I struggled to control the tears. I found it rather unpredictable, as a song I'd coped with one week, I suddenly couldn't cope with the next. It was the midweek service that I looked forward to.

With so many things being thrown at me, grieving often had to be put on hold. I was often too busy processing what was happening to process the loss. I had no space to grieve, and sometimes felt I was suppressing it, or blanking it out. When I did have time to process, it was short lived as it was soon interrupted by something else. I was feeling devastated and very raw. The desperate longing to be with Rick again was unbearable. I was still struggling to believe it had actually happened and trying to make sense of it. I discovered that it was hard to say goodbye to people I wasn't going to see for a while. I was afraid I might never see them again like Rick, so each parting was emotional for me.

One of the reasons that I often did not want to be with other people was that I didn't feel in control of my emotions. A friend described it as being like a vase filled to the brim. It would only take a slight nudge for it to overflow. At other times though, I felt totally dead inside, and as if my brain refused to dwell on Rick and what had happened, and I was therefore unable to feel the emotions. This felt like a strange place to be, and it concerned me if it continued for a while. I felt guilty that I was shutting him out. Sometimes this happened as a result of having to deal with other issues, but at other times I think I just couldn't cope with the intensity of all that I was feeling, and I shut down. The majority of the time though, I felt a huge sense of loss and grief.

Knowing that something might trigger grief put me on my guard. I could usually manage it with a lot of effort, but better still such a situation was to be avoided. Harder to deal with were the many things that took me by surprise and triggered grief. Some of these were ridiculous like a rubbish bin. Rick had cleared his bedroom out when he moved into a house, but his bin was still there. I'd been in and out of the room without noticing it. Then one day it caught my eye, and I remembered how I used to get annoyed at having to pick up all the rubbish from round the outside. The thought struck me that I'd give anything to be doing that now, and I sat and cried by the rubbish bin. There were so many other things that reminded me of Rick: places, phrases he used, people's mannerisms, a laugh that sounded like his, things he enjoyed or disliked. I would often think of things that I wanted to tell Rick or ask him, and then remember that I couldn't.

It seemed there were endless triggers, and it was worse when they happened in public. Classes from the local schools sometimes attended the communion service at the Anglican Church. They would sing a song during the service, and I was always rather apprehensive about which it might be. On one occasion, they sang with a CD and I didn't recognise the introduction, so I thought it was going to be all right. I suddenly registered they were singing a song that Rick had introduced to the holiday club, and which was the one that I most associated with him. I could see him doing the actions with the children, and I felt overwhelmed by the pain. I left the church and walked back to the car shaking and crying. I probably shouldn't have driven, but I needed to find a private place to deal with the pain and grief.

Although the pain and the grief could feel overwhelming, in a strange way I welcomed them. It was as if I was expressing my love for Rick through the grief. I felt guilty about thinking of trying to move on because that felt like saying I didn't care, and I didn't love him that much. Holding on to the grief was like holding on to him. At the same time I was afraid of getting stuck, and I did know that I needed to let go, but it couldn't be done until I was ready.

Reading through my journal now, I'm not sure how I did survive that first year. The battering was relentless on top of the dreadful sense of loss. Sometimes several things would all come together, which left me reeling. At other times there would be a short space, but I felt as though things were hanging over me, and I never felt free of the stress and pressure. Over time I got to the point where I was just waiting for the next bad thing to happen. I would often feel it wasn't worth bothering to make any effort anymore, as I was only going to get knocked back again. My life felt very out of control. I sometimes felt plunged into despair, and as if I couldn't carry on, but God was there for me through this time, and he stopped me from being completely overwhelmed.

Chapter 5 - Boardwalks

E very now and again, we came across a short boardwalk over the bog through the rushes. It was encouraging, and reassuring to come across these as, apart from the posts, they were the only times that we were sure we were on the right path. It was hard, however, to see why they were any more necessary over one part of the bog, than any other part. A boardwalk over the whole route would have been good! Nevertheless they were a respite, and we were grateful for these short stretches of easy walking.

The boardwalks represent the positive things that helped me during that first year as I tried to find my way. God provided for me in different ways as I fought to negotiate all the things that were being thrown at us, never mind the grief and pain that were constant companions. I was grateful for these reassurances and the moments of respite.

God reassured me on various occasions of his presence with me. Although I didn't understand and nothing made sense, I knew he was with me in it. I often felt a stillness and a closeness to God in the communion service, and this strengthened me to carry on. These reassurances also came through his word. Extra special were the times when I had the motivation and concentration to meditate, and spend time in his presence, and I received encouragement and reassurance through that. These times were few and far between, but when I managed to focus they provided me with the courage to keep going.

One of these occasions was when I first tried to write an essay for my course. I sat with the question at the top of a blank sheet of paper for ages. I just couldn't begin, and I had no motivation to do so either. My bible reading notes suggested sitting with your hands cupped open and waiting on your lap, and asking God what he wanted to give you that day. The word 'determination' came into my mind, and I could feel God giving this to me. I was able to start the essay, and to my amazement the determination continued over the next few days, and I completed all the essays for that particular unit. This determination helped me to complete some more practical things too, which had seemed beyond me.

Another time, reflecting on the Exodus, I thought about what it must been like for Moses and the Israelites to experience the Passover, but then to be trapped between the Red Sea and the approaching Egyptians. They then experienced a dramatic rescue, but this was followed by having to face other difficulties in the wilderness. How hard it must have been for them, at times, to understand God's purposes, but in spite of their negative reactions as they struggled to cope, God was with them in it all. A verse that God used to reassure me was Deuteronomy 31:8, 'the Lord himself goes before you and will be with you; he will never leave you nor forsake you. Do not be afraid; do not be discouraged.' I was reminded of something said on a retreat I had previously attended; that when God says he will not forsake you, he means that he will not forsake you.

I was also often aware of God giving me his strength in a lot of the difficult situations I was facing. On the 14th June I wrote in my journal, 'I still marvel that in spite of everything I can feel this inner strength that I know comes from God. Even in my worst times I know he is there with me, a solid rock. I am so grateful to him for that.' At the beginning of August I read Psalm 73:26, 'My flesh and my heart may fail, but God is the strength of my heart and my portion for ever.' I became aware that

God had been 'the strength of my heart' for the last six months, but that I hadn't been trusting him for the medical tests, and so I wasn't allowing him to help me. I prayed for forgiveness and a change of attitude. The next day, whilst out on a walk, a verse from a village church notice board struck me, 'Surely God is my salvation; I will trust and not be afraid. The Lord, the Lord himself, is my strength and my defence, he has become my salvation' (Isaiah 12:2). God was giving me the reassurance that I needed. This happened again before I went for the MRI scan in October. A meditation on the feeding of the 5,000 gave me the reassurance that in the same way that God had given abundant food, he could give abundant peace and strength. I found this to be true.

God reached out to me through other people too. I had a very supportive GP, who gave me the reassurance that what I was experiencing, as a result of everything that was happening, was totally understandable, and I wasn't losing it. I had regular appointments with her, and I always felt better for them. They were especially helpful over Anna's situation and the medical tests; I was able to ask questions and get explanations. She helped me not to have too high an expectation of what I could manage, and to accept that the tiredness and lack of motivation were to be expected. She encouraged me to look after myself and to remember that it was still early days.

Also invaluable was God's provision of Veronica, who was the priest at the Anglican Church. The curate at the church, who had suggested the midweek communion services to me, had told her about my situation because he thought she would be someone who could support me. So the first time I went to the communion service, much to my surprise, she offered to visit me. My first impressions of her were that she was a gentle person and someone I felt I could talk to, so I gratefully accepted her offer. I hadn't been looking for support, but it was being provided. As time went on, I had reason to be very grateful that she had taken the initiative in this.

On her first visit she got to know everything that was going on, but fortunately it didn't frighten her off. She continued to see me on a regular basis, and I found I could be totally open with her and she simply accepted whatever I said. She was a good listener, and her questions helped me to process. I learnt to use the silences too to process with the safety of having someone with me. Talking really helped, and with the rate at which things were happening I always had plenty to talk about, and work through. I felt frustrated that a lot of it was about what was happening, rather than about Rick and processing the bereavement, but I valued her support to get through all of that too. She was reassuring and encouraging, and I eventually felt comfortable enough to be able to share my grief with her. It was a relief to be able to do so, although it took several months for me to reach that point.

Another provision was two books which I was given. I wasn't able to read much as I couldn't focus, but these books really helped me. The first was one that Veronica gave me on her first visit, which was a book of daily bible readings on bereavement.[1] It was written by someone who had lost their husband, but it helped to look at different aspects of bereavement in general. It meant I was able to think one aspect through rather than just going round in circles, which is where my thoughts usually led me. I had to think past all the things that were happening, and the feelings they were generating, which were a distraction, to focus on the loss. I used the questions she asked to guide my reflections, and writing the answers helped me to focus and process. I found it helped to write down the many things I was feeling as a result of the loss, and what

I was missing about Rick. Although it was a painful thing to do and a trigger for grief, it still felt positive to begin to face up to the feelings.

I also gained reassurance from the book. It helped to read that grief is personal and we need to be ourselves. We should not compare ourselves with others, which I had been doing and feeling a failure as a result. We all have our own responses and our own ways of coping. I quoted in my journal, 'You don't need to be "strong" – you just need to be real.'[2] Until I met Veronica my grief had been very private. I had avoided people and situations because I was afraid of losing control as the tears were often close to the surface, and I didn't want to talk about it. The exception to this were three close friends, whose support was invaluable, but even with them I still kept the grief under control, as I also did at first with Veronica. That was how I was and that was OK.

It was also reassuring to read that it is all right to cry out to God with the questions you have, and to express feelings like the psalmist. As the psalmist found, God can seem most distant when we have the greatest need of him. He isn't, but that is how it can feel and the questions can seem overwhelming. Again I found writing the questions down helped as did this statement, 'sharing our doubts and dilemmas with God is an act of honest faith.'[3] Even though I knew some of these things, it was freeing to read them in the context of the situation in which I found myself, and to apply them.

Some of it I wasn't ready for, either I didn't understand, or it felt beyond me. I struggled with the concept of a positive focus, but this quote I wrote in my journal gave me hope, 'We can keep trusting that we will feel better; indeed that we will learn and grow and emerge with new insights, qualities and skills for enriching our own and other people's lives.'[4] Recovery of any sort felt like a long way off, but it challenged me to think about whether I wanted to recover. It felt like a tall order, and for me at that point recovery felt like a betrayal of Rick. On the other hand I didn't want to get stuck as 'bereaved'. I realised I had to find my own way through it, and it would take as long as it took. Moving on couldn't be rushed, and getting stuck would be a lot further down the line, there was no pressure. This all helped me to believe that I could come through this a stronger person with a stronger faith. This possibility and hope for the future gave me strength.

The second book, Postcards from the Edge: Finding God in Hard Places (IVP), was written by Ian Coffey from Moorlands, and he gave us a copy when we went to visit Helen. He had dedicated it to Rick and that made it special, but it was also extremely relevant. It was about finding God in hard places and included chapters on loss, despair, courage, inadequacy, and doubt. I felt as though it had been written specifically for me and my situation! Obviously it hadn't, but it was certainly perfect timing. The chapter on loss was again reassuring and encouraging, as well as challenging. It helped to read that others found it hard to go back to church, which made it seem more acceptable. There was comfort in statements like, 'People respond to loss in different ways and because of this, the grieving process varies.'[5] I had previously begun reading a book that had seemed to me rather negative about grieving. I had been unable to finish it, and it had left me rather confused, so it was a relief to read this, 'Grieving is part of being human, and to deny or suppress it as being unspiritual is as daft as it is dangerous.'[6] This was followed by the reminder that as Christians our grief is with hope, because of Jesus' resurrection it is not the end. The final challenge at the end of this chapter was to do something good with the pain.

However, it was the chapter on despair that had the greatest impact. I was at a point where an accumulation of events had left me feeling very low. I forced myself to go to the midweek communion, where we were encouraged to engage with our emotions during the intercessions. This sounded like dangerous ground to me! Instead of switching off I managed to go along with it, and God used the intercessions to show me that I had reached a point of despair. This solved nothing, but somehow it helped to identify what it was I needed to deal with. I drove home thinking I needed someone to talk to. When I arrived home a wise and trusted friend rang me, and I was able to go and see her and talk through all that had happened over recent days, which helped. I felt God had provided for me and met my need, but there was more to come.

I decided to read the chapter on despair, which described how Elijah reached that point after his amazing experience on Mount Carmel, and how God dealt with him. God provided for Elijah at every point of his need. This included physically, mentally, and emotionally as he journeyed towards Horeb, where he met with God in a new way. I drew encouragement from the chapter's conclusion to Elijah's story, 'Elijah experienced despair, and I shouldn't be surprised if there are times when I face the same. God met Elijah in his darkest time, and I can trust God to do the same for me.'[7] Over the next few days I was to find how true this was.

At this stage Anna was in hospital and we were told she would be there for the next week. With Elijah's experience in mind, I became convinced that I needed to go away. We hadn't had a holiday for a year, and this seemed a good opportunity. Unfortunately David didn't share my need to get away, and there were a number of factors which made it difficult for us to go. Not least of these was the effort involved in finding and booking somewhere. When you are drained and exhausted anything feels like too much effort, even doing things that might help. It was at this point that God provided for us. A friend from church rang and asked if we would like to use their lodge in Wales for a few days. David cleared it at work, and we were able to gratefully accept.

Not only did God provide us with the lodge, which was in a lovely situation, but he provided us with the weather too. On the 9th September I wrote in my journal, 'This is absolutely idyllic sitting on the veranda looking out over the wonderful view with the top of the low cliffs, the blue sea and the land and mountains beyond.' There was something healing about simply sitting and looking at that view. We did a lot of walking too, a total of 23 miles over three days. It was a chance for us to talk, time to reflect, to unwind, and to gain a fresh perspective. It was wonderful to be able to be outside for so much of the day, from breakfast to early evening, and the sun, sea, and creation all brought me to a better place. As with Elijah, I felt God had met me at every point of my need, and the despair had lifted.

It had done me so much good that the following Sunday morning I went back to church. As I'd thought about Elijah's experience, I'd remembered he had returned at the end of it, and I'd felt that it was time for me to return to church. I found it hard to go, but as I walked into the church God provided for me again as I felt an inner strength, which I knew came from him, and which got me through. God had also shown Elijah that his situation was not as dire as he had supposed. There were 7,000 others in Israel who continued to worship him and not Baal, so Elijah was not alone. On our return home, we found that we were no longer on our own in the situation with Anna. This was the point where a psychiatrist was starting to do something for her. We didn't know where we were going with this, but we had hope.

A further way which God provided for us, during this first year, was a Support Day for bereaved parents. This was run by Care for the Family in November. It seemed a good idea when we booked to go, but as the day got closer I became rather apprehensive. I wasn't at all sure what to expect, or why I was going, or how it could possibly help. Above all could I cope with it? Helen had been on a weekend they had run for young widows, and she had found it helpful, which was what had encouraged me to agree to go. Although I'd read about bereavement in general, I hadn't read anything about the loss of a child. My initial reaction on arrival was what a relief it was to be with people who shared that experience. Although our circumstances were all different, as were our ways of coping, we had all experienced the same devastating loss. There was a depth of understanding that only those who have been through that can share.

We were divided into groups with those whose situations were similar. Our group consisted of those who had lost children who were adults. Our first task was to fill in a spider diagram. I struggled with this as it included memories. Thinking of memories was still too painful for me and I couldn't do it without tears, so I gave up on that one. We shared our stories in our groups, and although it was tough hearing what other people had been through, it made me feel less on my own. I was a bit surprised when it got to our turn to share and David said, 'you do it.' I hadn't expected that, and I'd been so engaged with everyone else's story I hadn't begun to think how to tell our story. I muddled my way through and struggled to keep going at points, but it felt good to have done it.

One of the things I found most helpful, was an illustration they used to show that the loss stays the same size, but your capacity to cope gets larger. This was a defining moment for me, as I realised that moving on doesn't minimise the loss in any way. The loss won't ever change, but I have to learn to live with it. We were introduced to the concept of finding a new 'normal.' It's not what we want, or what we would choose, but will eventually happen. A husband and wife shared how they dealt with their loss in different ways. As David and I seemed to be poles apart in dealing with it, I found this both helpful and reassuring. Their approach to significant days, like anniversaries, was very different, and I think it helped David to understand why it wasn't just like any other day for me. Altogether it was a very positive day, and I gained hope for the future from people whose loss was longer ago than ours.

In January God also provided me with an opportunity which meant a lot to me. David was preaching in the morning service, and this also involved doing a children's talk. I made the mistake of telling him that I knew how I would do it. The next thing I knew, I was down to do the talk with no recollection of actually agreeing to it! The service was a week before the anniversary of Rick's death, and as I prayed about the talk it seemed appropriate to do it as I knew it was something he would have encouraged me to do. He supported and encouraged me so much with the children's work, so it felt as if it would be a tribute to him and what he did for me. I was grateful to God for giving me this opportunity, but I knew I could only do it in his strength, and I needed him to take over as he had done in the past. He did as I walked to the front, and I felt relaxed and enjoyed doing it, which was amazing considering the bad week I'd had beforehand. People's comments afterwards made me feel that it had been a fitting tribute, and I was so glad I'd stepped out in faith and God had provided for me.

These boardwalks of God's provision, as on the walk, were only a temporary relief, and I was soon stepping off into the bog again. Having something firm under my feet for even a short space of time, however, was what got me through that first year. God met my needs, and gave me the encouragement, reassurance, and hope that made survival possible.

Chapter 6 - The steep narrow path

W hat a relief to reach the path out of the bog! Again, however, the relief was only temporary. I started with enthusiasm, only to discover that although the path was easy to follow, it was steep and extremely narrow with a drop to our right. It was difficult walking in a different way. I was afraid of losing my balance, and I had to keep stopping to catch my breath.

There was something about surviving the first year. We had got through all the 'firsts' of everything like the birthdays, Christmas, and the anniversary of Rick's death. I emerged feeling battered from all that we had been through, but hopeful for a bit of respite. We had completed all the tests, and Anna was safe and receiving treatment in a residential setting. We had reached the path out of the bog. We soon discovered, however, that the path was to be difficult in a different way as we continued to be battered, and each thing caused us to stop to catch our breath before we could carry on. There were times when I felt very close to going over the edge.

In the same way that I started the path out of the bog with enthusiasm, which quickly receded, I discovered that I wasn't as ready to engage with life again, after the scare with my lung, as I thought I was. After the initial relief, it took a while to get over the stress it had created, and I felt very fragile. A lot of the time I was barely functioning, although every now and again I could push myself to achieve more. One of my main motivations for keeping going had been for Anna and David's sake. Anna had now gone away and David seemed in a better place, so I'd lost that motivation. It became all too easy not to make an effort, there seemed to be no point. Fortunately I had times where my mood lifted and I was able to feel more positive, but I felt in need of some space.

There were a couple of pictures that gave me hope at this time. A brown twig looks dead, but has the potential for life to come. As we approached spring, there was evidence of this new life emerging. A dead twig felt like a good description of how I was feeling, but it was encouraging to think that God could bring back life in me.[1] The other picture was of a butterfly, which has to go through the chrysalis stage and enter 'oblivion,' in order for a complete transformation to take place. In the same way God can bring us through the wilderness and transform us. We have to trust him to make one small change at a time, and we have to be prepared to accept and go along with the changes.[2] These were positive things to reflect on, and I felt peaceful about patiently waiting for God to bring about changes.

It was when we discovered that Anna wasn't as settled as we thought on the unit, and wanted to leave, that I realised how close to the edge I was. I knew I'd been getting stressed very easily and over reacting in various situations, but now I really felt that I couldn't cope. I felt that I had nothing to give to her, and I was running on empty. We went to visit her and tried to encourage her to keep going with it, and came home exhausted. On top of this, I was not letting myself think about Rick, and I felt dead inside. My GP asked if I thought this was all sustainable. When I said no, she suggested bereavement counselling. This simply added to my stress as it was something I couldn't face doing. On the other hand, I was worried that the GP thought I was at a point where it was necessary because I was stuck. Was counselling really the way God wanted to bring about changes? I had thought it was about having some space and allowing God to take me forward. Other people had seemed to think rest and space were what I needed. I was in no state to make the decision. I eventually realised that not going down the counselling route for the time being was all right, I could always do it in the future. The question then was how long to give it. It was stressful frequently wondering if I was doing the right thing.

I had to wait a while before I got any space. During that wait, I was really struggling with physical exhaustion. On top of that, whilst talking to Veronica, a memory came back very strongly, which was a trigger for grief. It was a shock to go from feeling nothing to being overwhelmed by grief. I certainly wasn't stuck in the feeling of deadness anymore, and the tears were, once again, constantly very close to the surface. I felt a physical and emotional wreck. I'd also been informed, a while before, that the course I was doing was to be discontinued. I sent off my last assessment, and although it had at times been a pressure, it was one more thing I'd lost, which made my life even emptier. I was still managing to go to church, but one Sunday morning I could not cope with the sermon. It was more the implication of what was being said, when applied to our situation, that I was too vulnerable to cope with. Although there was part of me that thought I didn't agree with what had been said, I wasn't capable of thinking it through. It seemed so hard and cold, and I felt as though I'd lost God. I was now a spiritual wreck too. Also the pressure of the question of Anna's future was now continual, with a lack of consistency in the way she was being treated, and with no explanations.

By the time I got the longed for space, I was not in a place to use it. I could not spend time with God in the way I'd wanted to, I easily became overwhelmed by grief, and I didn't have the energy or motivation to be creative, or to go for a walk. It wasn't the time out I'd planned, and the best that can be said for it was that I got a bit of rest. I did manage to do some reading to try and sort out my thoughts following the sermon, which helped. This time was followed by a week's holiday in Worcestershire. We had a lovely cottage, which was in a beautiful area with fantastic views, and I found them healing, but at the same time I was struggling. We had some lovely walks, but I was continually fighting against low energy levels, which spoilt my enjoyment of them. I was surprised to find how hard it was to cope with being away from home this time. David wasn't well at the beginning of the holiday, which threw me when I felt so fragile and vulnerable. I wondered how I was going to survive the week, but things improved and I did return feeling better than before I went.

Although we had the continual concern over Anna, we entered a more settled phase for the next few weeks. I was able to do more reading and processing, and I felt closer to God again as I received more encouragement. I was drawn towards being open to what God was trying to teach me through this time. As often happens, this was brought to my attention in various ways. One of these was thinking about the comparison of our lives to the ebb and flow of the tide. The ebbs are those circumstances in our lives that we would not have chosen. They can, however, be positive times when God reveals things to us, in the same way that the ebb of the tide reveals things hidden in the flow. If we let them be, they can be periods of growth.[3]

I was experiencing waves of pain and grief, but they were not as frequent, something I felt guilty about as it seemed as though I no longer cared. I then had a significant moment with a realisation that removed the guilt. I couldn't have Rick back, which was what I really wanted, and I had got to carry on without him, but I didn't have to feel guilty about doing so because he was in my heart. He had a special place there, and that would never change. This may seem obvious, but I had to come to know, at a deep level, the truth of it for myself, and how it affected my life. It was a conviction that was special and freeing. Moments of realisation are something that I have experienced more than once since Rick died, and they lead to an awareness that something has fallen into a more comfortable place. Missing Rick, the pain and the grief were still there, but I was no longer concerned about the times I was not so aware of them. My capacity to cope had increased.

Another issue which caused guilt for me was that I no longer felt able to go to church on a Sunday morning. I was feeling more and more drawn towards the Anglican Church. I went there on a few Sunday mornings as well as to the midweek communion, but I felt guilty that I wasn't going to the church where I was a member and David was an Elder. I had a sense of duty that was stopping me from moving on. This was a dilemma for me that lasted a long time. I also felt guilty that I wasn't 'doing' anything in either church. So when I got the opportunity to run the children's group again for six weeks, while the couple who had taken over from me were away, I jumped at the chance. As the time for me to do this got closer, I decided it might not have been such a good idea! I found it very hard to prepare as that involved making decisions, I had no confidence in what I was doing, and I felt out of my depth. You wouldn't have thought that it was something I'd done for seven years! I got there in the end, and it was a good job that I had planned it all. I only managed to do two of the weeks before we entered another phase of battering, and I had to hand it over.

On a Sunday in June I started experiencing abdominal pain. By Tuesday evening, I was in hospital having my appendix removed. Certainly hadn't seen that one coming! It was the first operation I had ever had, but I felt very calm about it all. It was just the next thing that was happening to me. I couldn't believe how well I felt the day after the operation, but then it all deteriorated and I was very unwell for several days. I became desperate to leave the hospital with its constant noise. Eventually I was well enough to go, but I was exhausted and very weak. So began the slow process of recovery.

As is often the case, physical exhaustion had an effect on me mentally, emotionally, and spiritually. I felt very detached from everything, as though I was floating around in a bubble. Every now and again I would bump into aspects of my life, e.g. Rick's birthday, or a visit by Anna. These were all in separate bubbles, and I couldn't really engage with any of it. I'd bump into it, and just float away again. I did, however, find some fight from somewhere. My aim was to get back to managing by myself, and to doing things around the house, so that David wouldn't have to do them. He was very busy at this point with various things, and I didn't want to stop him being able to do them. I didn't want to see anyone, my concentration was poor, I kept needing to rest, and I was struggling with conversations, both with others and God. I went out with David to our local shops, and I really struggled to cope. It all seemed so busy, and I didn't have the strength to hurry across the car park. I felt very weak and vulnerable, and feeling that bad totally took my confidence. I continued to work on building up my strength, but it was a long, slow process. I was easily thrown by little things going wrong, and they triggered strong reactions that were out of proportion.

By the end of July, I was strong enough for us to go and stay with my mother in Sussex for a week. It was such a relief to go away, and to have a relaxed time with some lovely gentle walks. It was a respite, but I found it very hard to go back. I was still struggling to manage physically, and I still didn't want to see anyone. I was worried about what was happening with Anna, as they were talking about discharging her, but I wasn't sure a great deal had changed. It felt as if they were giving up on her, and I couldn't face going back to where we had been. I was missing Rick's ability to cheer me up, and I couldn't be bothered with God. The days felt very empty, and I became very low. Each time I pushed myself to try something, and then felt I wasn't managing, my confidence went even lower.

My GP was very reassuring that all this was understandable, given what I'd been through. She thought my brain was malfunctioning, and suggested that I should find something practical to do to distract myself. One of her suggestions was gardening, a suggestion that David thoroughly approved of! The garden was something I mostly left to him, but he had been too busy to do much for a while. As a result there was plenty to do. So much in fact, I felt rather overwhelmed by it, and I wasn't sure I had the strength to tackle it. David kindly provided me with a list of jobs, so I started doing a little bit at a time, and I found it helped. The visit to the doctors had also taken the pressure off in other ways. I stopped trying to do things when I didn't feel able to. I concentrated instead on doing what I could, when I could. I totally lost it with David when he tried to get me to do something I felt I couldn't, but that led to me telling him about the conversation with the doctor, and that I was tired of pretending I was all right, when I wasn't. A few days later, I regretted telling him this.

On the 20th August, David's Dad was suddenly taken ill in the evening and rushed into hospital. This coincided with the first time that Anna had been allowed an overnight stay with us. We went to be with David's Mum, who was very agitated, while he went to the hospital. His Mum calmed down, but refused to go to bed, so we sat up with her, and once she fell asleep I spent the time wondering where we were going with this. David's Dad was the carer for his Mum who had been diagnosed with Alzheimers. David eventually returned at 4.45am, when his Dad had been taken to a ward. We managed to persuade his Mum to go to bed, and David stayed with her. Anna and I went home to bed, but I only managed to doze for an hour. I tried to rest, but I was too worked up, so I gave up and got up. I was worried about Anna coping with it, and very concerned about both of David's parents, and so our next stressful time began.

It was sad visiting David's Dad who, from managing very well at the age of 95, had suddenly become very confused, and didn't seem to know what was happening. It was so hard when we left and he tried to come with us. He deteriorated rapidly as the list of things wrong with him increased, and visits became very difficult as we witnessed this. After nearly three weeks in hospital, there was nothing more that they could do for him, and sadly he passed away. Having to tell David's Mum was one of the hardest things I've ever had to do; they were everything to each other. She refused to believe us and was convinced, if she went to see him, she could persuade him to wake up. She insisted on going to see him, so we took her, but she was still struggling to take it in. Quite understandably, she did not want to believe it.

When David's Dad went into hospital, we took over as his Mum's carers. We muddled through while he was in hospital. They lived close by, so I was going across several times a day to help her, and David was sleeping there each night. Hospital visits were not easy as she could not walk far, so we had to wait for a wheelchair to be available to take her up to the ward. We had barely been managing one house and garden, now we had two to look after. When his Dad died, we realised this wasn't sustainable, so started to look at care homes. We wanted to get her name on a waiting list as soon as possible as we were expecting a long wait. I hated doing it behind her back, but she had enough to cope with as she continued to struggle to believe what had happened. She could be completely lucid at times and very confused and rambling at others. All we could do was try to support her as best we could. On top of this we obviously had a funeral to arrange, and everything else you have to do following a death. Anna was a great support when she came at the weekends, but then she began to struggle again so couldn't come, and there was no more talk of her being discharged.

We were feeling very stretched. My main concern was to support David; I hated seeing him having to go through this. Having just told him how low I was feeling, I wanted him to see that I was managing so that I wasn't an extra pressure, and someone else for him to be concerned about. As I was in a position where I had to do things I didn't feel able to do, I had to fight my lack of confidence, I was dragging myself through each day, but I was coping. It would have been nice though, if I could have properly got over one thing before the next bad thing happened. Another problem, in the middle of all this, was that my car failed its MOT, and we were sure the same would be true of Anna's. So we had to take time out to replace them. Fortunately we managed it quickly, but it was a further drain on our time and energy.

David's parents, especially his Dad, were bad at getting rid of things, and the prospect of having to clear the house was rather overwhelming. He had been fairly organised with his paperwork, but he had kept most of it! We even found a receipt for a camera from the 1950's, and other documents from before that! However, we were constantly struggling to find the pieces of paper we actually needed as they were in random places. We eventually discovered his mother's birth certificate amongst recipes, cut out from magazines, in a drawer in the kitchen! The garage was full of things that had been kept in case they were needed. David had to cut back on his busyness in order to deal with all of this. He had known that our cars were an issue, but he had not had time to deal with it until he suddenly had to, and I think he began to realise he had been too busy. Working more hours and getting involved in a lot of things at church had been his way of coping, but it had led to other things being neglected.

It was a relief to get the other side of the funeral. I still didn't want to be with people, so this was a challenge, but I felt very calm on the day. I had a strange moment towards the end of the service where I just shut down. When I came to, I didn't know where we were in the service, and David had to tell me it was time to leave. I felt disorientated and rather disconcerted by what had happened.

Looking after David's mother continued to be a challenge. The hardest thing was trying to get her to eat. She kept going 'off' things, and she wasn't 'on' much in the first place. It could be very frustrating. Shortly after the funeral, we had a call from a care home saying they had a place. This felt too soon, but we didn't want to let it go. His mother wanted to stay at home, so we had to explain why we couldn't manage that, and she seemed to become resigned to the move. I hated leaving her at the home on the day we moved her in. We had a slightly rocky start during which she told the manager he wasn't fit to run a care home, and she'd call the BBC and get them to run a documentary about him. He'd heard it all before! By the third day she was telling us what a wonderful place the home was. It was lovely to watch her settling in so well, and we felt as though a weight had been lifted.

We continued to work at clearing out the house. A more interesting aspect was getting some things valued and sold at auction, but mostly it was endless trips to a charity shop and the tip. To our surprise, the Estate Agent found a buyer for the house without it actually going on the market. Now we had a deadline to work to, but we were struggling to stay motivated. I was getting concerned about David. I'd never seen him like this before; it was like something had gone out of him. Also Anna was not at all well through this time, and I often felt on overload. At times David and I worked well together, at others it got rather fraught. We were both feeling the pressure. Once the house was cleared it was going to need a thorough clean, and I couldn't see how we were going to get it done in time.

On top of this, after celebrating her 90th birthday, in January David's mother began a rapid decline. We had been visiting her daily, and although she'd had bad days, she'd seemed very settled. It was as if she suddenly gave up. She was barely eating or drinking and no longer left her room. Our visits became times of trying to reason with her to get her to drink, but I'm not sure she was capable of processing. She would agree with everything we said and then still refuse to drink. It was so hard to watch her deteriorating in this way, and to be totally unable to help her. By the beginning of March we'd moved to end of life care, and a few days later she passed away.

We didn't get a chance to draw breath though. We had finished sorting the house, but the sale hadn't gone through as soon as expected. This left us with the issue of needing to sort out probate as quickly as possible, so as not to hold up the sale for too long. Unfortunately, probate and inheritance tax don't happen quickly, no matter how hard you try. We had to wait two weeks just to get a reference number. We were also arranging a funeral, only six months after the last one.

Having got through the funeral, we had a day and a half before being hit by the next crisis. Allegations had been made against Anna, and she was being discharged and was coming home. We were in no place to handle this, but I had to make several phone calls to try to find out what was happening. Eventually, it was decided she would just come for the weekend. After more phone calls, it was established that the allegations were false and had been withdrawn. They had caused a great deal of distress to all of us, but for now Anna was back on the unit. Finally by the beginning of May, we had probate and the sale went through. David bounced back quickly once the pressure was off, but that wasn't the case for me. I'd fought my way to the top of the hill without going over the edge, but I was not in a good place.

Chapter 7 - Tree stumps

When we reached the top of the hill, we found that the next part of the walk was littered with obstacles. A forest area had been felled, and the tree stumps remained. We had to balance along the top of the furrows between each tree stump as the bottom was full of water; once again we were in a boggy area. This meant we couldn't get round the tree stumps on our path, but had to go over them. They were slippery and at an angle, so hard to negotiate. We were going downhill, and at the bottom, some of the felled trees had been left behind. These were easier for David than for me. Being shorter, I found it harder to clamber over them.

The tree stumps represent the harder than normal days that have to be negotiated, like Christmas and birthdays. The felled trees symbolise the even harder days, the anniversaries of Rick's death. The furrows represent the time leading up to these days. I found the anticipation and trying to decide what to do on these days was difficult in itself. So too was the time immediately afterwards. The initial feeling was one of relief that the day was over, followed by the realisation that nothing had changed, and the loss with its pain and grief were as bad as ever. These obstacles were only one section of the walk, but on my journey through thick and thin they obviously occurred at regular intervals. They would pull me down, and make it even harder to cope with what was happening.

In the same way that the stumps and the felled trees were easier for David to negotiate than for me, so were these hard days. His way of coping with them would have been to carry on and treat them as a normal day, whereas I felt the need to mark some of them in some way. We both respected where the other was coming from, but it felt like an added complication. I did not want to impose what I needed to do on him, but he wanted to support me. I found it hard to accept this as I felt it was 'our' hard day, not 'my' hard day, and he shouldn't have to support me. So I encouraged him to carry on as normal and tried to do my own thing as much as possible.

Some tree stumps were easier than others. Although they were days of more intense sadness, I found that I could use distractions, and it was a case of getting through them. These included Mother's Day, Easter and my birthday. They were times when I would have heard from Rick, but he would not have been with us. Much harder were the times when we would have seen him. Christmas became, as it is for many, a time to dread and something I had to drag myself through. It wasn't so much the day itself, as Rick wouldn't have been with us, but the week following when we would definitely have had him and Helen staying at some point. It seemed a never ending time to get through.

The first Christmas, I wore one of his rings on a chain round my neck every day. I felt the need to have something of his close to me. I haven't felt the need to do that since; the things I needed to do changed with time. I desperately wanted to do something that would make the Christmas period different in some way, like going away, but our circumstances were such that I couldn't see a way to make changes. I just wanted to ignore it, but that wasn't an option either. It helped to do something positive by giving the money, which we would have spent on Rick's present, to a charity we knew he would have supported.

I found the Christmas cards hard to cope with. They fell into three categories. The first was from those who carried on as though nothing had happened, and they hurt. The second was from people who sent a card saying Merry Christmas, but acknowledged that it would be hard. This was better, but I didn't understand why they had chosen a card saying Merry Christmas in the first place. The third category had a more suitable message, with words added by the sender that showed they cared and were thinking of us, and those I could cope with. The Christmas tree was another issue for me. A few years previously I'd complained about our tree decorations. In typical Rick fashion he'd immediately set about putting that right for me, and took me to choose new ones. To have had those in the lounge would have been far too painful, so I was very glad when David decided he couldn't be bothered to put the tree up. I also didn't want to go outside after dark. Rick and I used to go for a walk to look at the lights and decorations outside people's houses, and these now reduced me to tears.

On Christmas Day, I was surprised that I was able to engage with what Christmas is really about. I lit a candle and thought about Jesus as light in the darkness, and what that meant amongst all the pain and grief. I found God's comfort through this reflection. God gave me the peace and strength to survive Christmas Day, but the following week seemed to be interminable. We were approaching New Year, and I had realised that this was an issue for me. By moving into 2016 I felt as though I was leaving Rick behind in 2015, and I didn't know how to handle that. I knew I needed to do something significant as the feeling was so strong. A friend had given me a candle, and I eventually worked out that I needed to light that at midnight, as a symbol that I was taking Rick with me into 2016. It was a relief to know what it was that I needed to do. The candle did help me to focus on the fact that I wasn't leaving him behind, and I was certainly aware that the pain and grief were coming with me into the next year. It meant that the next day, I could write in my journal that I now felt peaceful about being in 2016. Sometimes the significant things I needed to do were fairly simple, but nonetheless very meaningful. Again I have not felt the need to repeat this at New Year.

The second Christmas didn't seem any easier. On the 19th December 2016 I wrote in my journal, 'Been struggling so much with missing Rick. Christmas makes everything so much harder, a time when we would definitely have seen him. Constant Christmas cards wishing us a happy Christmas don't help – how is it going to be happy?' Visiting David's mother in the home on Christmas Day made it different, which helped, but Boxing Day was another matter. I was on my own at home for a short time, which was fine until it suddenly hit me that it was about the time Rick and Helen would have been arriving, and I was overwhelmed by the sense of loss. It wasn't until the next year that we were able to do what I knew I'd needed to do, to go away for Christmas. We went to my mothers, and it made it much easier to cope with. The feelings of missing Rick and longing to see him were still there, but were not so intense in a different place, and it was easier to distract myself. Christmas remained a hard time, and always will do, but I had found the key to making it more manageable.

The birthdays, in the summer, were also one of the harder tree stumps to negotiate. Rick's, Anna's, and David's birthdays happened in the space of eight days, and Rick had always been with us at some point over this time. Cards were again an issue for me, but this time it was buying them that was the problem. Buying two cards instead of three hit me hard every year. Also the cards with 'Son' on would always jump out at me, even though I tried hard to avoid them. I eventually found a simple adjustment to make this easier. I didn't buy the cards until after what would have been Rick's birthday, and it felt better doing it past the time I would have bought one for him.

The first year was the hardest in the sense of knowing what to do on the day. After much thought, we settled on giving what would have been his birthday present to charity. We wanted to give it to somewhere that was personal to Rick, and Moorlands was the obvious choice. This became the significant thing we did each year. Apart from that, it was using distractions to get through the day. I could not believe how much time slowed down on these days, and it was exhausting trying to fill them with different activities. For the other birthdays, including mine in the autumn, we supported each other and tried to find different things to do. Our 60th birthdays were hard as Rick would have been involved in those. On top of missing Rick, I spent my 60th getting David's mother's things ready for her move to the home the next day, which I was dreading. It was definitely the worst birthday I had ever had.

Other tree stumps were one off events, including weddings. Thinking of Rick's friend getting married without his best man was a very sad day, especially as it was less than two months after Rick's death. I was glad they had gone ahead with it, but I really felt for them. Our nephew's wedding was in the summer of 2015, and it was important to us to be there. As we'd had two family weddings the year before, including Rick and Helens, which were both special times it made this one all the harder. Although it brought back memories, I tried to focus on the day being about the bride and groom, and pushed other thoughts into the background. It was a special occasion, but for me it was bittersweet. I was pleased that I'd managed it, and coped with being with the wider family in spite of it accentuating the pain of loss. Sadly, we had to decline all further wedding invitations from his peer group at church; I just couldn't face them. There was a limit to what I could push myself through, and I was grateful that everyone was very understanding.

Then we come to the felled trees, the anniversaries of Rick's death. I started dreading these almost as soon as the Christmas period was over. For me, at first, these needed to be all about Rick. My longing to see him was so intense it was almost unbearable. Distractions didn't work as I felt guilty thinking about anything else. I certainly made them harder for myself than was necessary, but at first it was what I needed to do. How to do this each year was a problem, and it was always a relief to have worked something out, although this often didn't happen until quite close to the day. This was also a time when I relived all that happened around the time of his death. I didn't want to, but it would keep replaying in my head, it was all so vivid. These anniversaries seemed too much to cope with on top of all the other things we were going through.

For the first anniversary, I decided that making bread was a fitting thing to do as it was something we had done together. This didn't feel like enough, and Veronica suggested I should use the bread in some way. She offered to come and take a communion service for us. This was the answer I had been looking for. I invited three close friends, who had supported me so well through the year, to share in this with us. Making and shaping the bread rolls was good therapy and was absorbing, which helped me through the morning. The communion service was very special, and it was a lovely setting in which to remember Rick. For me though, this day was made far harder by the uncertainty caused by the results of the MRI scan.

The second anniversary was the beginning of being able to tackle the photos of Rick. After two years I had still been unable to look at any, and therefore we had none of him displayed. I decided the time had come to change that; I would choose twelve photos to go in a frame to stand on the hearth in the lounge. The frame contained pictures of his wedding, so removing those was tough in itself. I made my choice of photos, and then the actual process of putting them in the frame was a challenge, which absorbed me for quite a while! I was glad I'd managed to do it; it felt like something special to have done and a big step forward for me. I did struggle with having it in the lounge though; I found it could catch me unawares. One small photo in a corner might have been a more sensible way to start! The rest of the day was a struggle. Talking to Veronica about all the memories, which were replaying in my head, helped them to recede a bit. Even going for a walk later, which usually helped my mood, did not help with all I was feeling on that day.

Veronica supported me again on the third anniversary. We watched the DVD of the speeches, and the first dance at Rick and Helen's wedding. It was so lovely to see Rick, but so painful. Some of the things that were said about their future together were very hard to hear. I got lost in it at points, and it was so difficult when it was finished to come back to reality. I was glad in a way that I'd watched it, but I was struggling to cope with the pictures I was left with of him being so alive. I couldn't work out what I wanted to do next. I didn't want to be at home, and I wanted to leave David to deal with the day in his own way. I decided to go to the Anglican Church and light a candle. As I looked at the candle, I was very tearful as I thought about how much I loved Rick. I couldn't focus enough to pray, but I found comfort in looking at the vases of daffodils, which were brightening up the space, and gave me hope. As I left, I felt the need to go and be with a friend, and a mixture of talking about Rick and other things with her, helped me to feel a bit better.

After this, I managed to find a different way of handling these days. The Anglican Church held a service on All Souls Day in November. Rick's name had been read out at these services, but I had not felt ready to go to them. I plucked up the courage to go and found it a very gentle, special time of remembering Rick. When I came to the next anniversary, this service inspired me to spend time remembering Rick in a positive way, and giving thanks for him. I lit the candle I'd used on the first New Year in memory of Rick, and as I thought about him I thanked God for him. It was very emotional, but positive. Along with this, I was able to lay down the memories of the time of his death, which had gripped me. I felt freed from my feeling that the day ought to be devoted to Rick, and it was disloyal to do anything else. I thought about Rick a lot of the time anyway, so a certain day didn't need to be that intense. I found that, for the first time, I didn't need other people to help me to get through the day. These days are still felled trees, but I'm climbing over them a bit more easily.

Although all these days were hard, I found on more than one occasion that I was actually more receptive to things God was trying to show me. This meant that some of these days included a positive experience, and I was able to move forward in some way. I was always aware that God was with me in them, and he gave me his peace and comfort. He also provided me with people when I needed them. I was aware too that people were praying for me as I felt upheld on these difficult days.

It was whilst walking through the area of felled trees that we met some people going the other way. We had not met any other people since near the beginning of the walk. I could understand why! They told us it wasn't far to the track we needed to take us up the hill. This was so encouraging that for a short way we felt re-energised. This soon changed to disillusionment as not far seemed to be going on for a very long time.

I found that things people said to me, their responses, and reactions had quite an impact on me whilst I was in such a vulnerable state. I realise it is hard for people to know what to do or say. I understand that, and I'm not judging or criticising them. It was simply that some things encouraged me, others triggered guilt or grief, and others made me feel set apart. Also there were some questions I didn't know how to answer. I was constantly concerned about the impression I was giving and how I 'should be'. This is reflected in my journal entry on 12th of April 2015, 'How should I be behaving? What should I be doing or not doing? Are people going to feel I don't care if I do so and so? Should I be able to enjoy going for a walk? Should I be able to feel pleasure in God's creation or should I feel guilty about feeling that? Can I laugh without feeling guilty? Given Rick's sense of humour would he really have wanted us to stop laughing?'

On the same day, I wrote this about people's responses, 'I can't cope with everyone's sympathy. I can't cope if people try to avoid me. I can't cope with making people feel uncomfortable because I'm there and they don't know what to say or do.' The conclusion I came to was that it was so much easier just being by myself. This was part of my reason for withdrawing as much as I did. An example of one of the things that made me want to retreat was the day that I was leaving Tesco with my shopping, and someone I knew was coming in. The look of panic on his face when he saw me made me wish the floor would open up and swallow me. I hated making people feel like that. I took evasive action by giving the trolley a huge shove, and calling out hello as I went past him at speed. The problem then was getting the trolley back under control as it picked up more speed down the slope towards the oncoming traffic!

There were, however, many positive reactions. One that stands out for me was a friend who came to visit me. She gave me some flowers and a hug then left. She had said all that needed to be said without words, and that meant a lot to me. When I returned to running the children's group, I got such a lovely welcome back from a leader it really boosted my confidence. Another leader had recently lost her mother, and she just said, 'let's have a hug,' followed by, 'there that's over, now let's get on.' That was perfect for me, we had shown we cared about each other, but there was no fuss, and we just got on with what we were there to do. Someone simply telling me that they were praying for me was always encouraging. There were far more positives than negatives, but being sensitive the negatives had a greater impact.

I found that other people moved on fairly quickly, and how I 'should be' became less of an issue over time. I was surprised, though, how soon I too was expected to move on. I quickly realised that I was supposed to say that I was all right when asked how I was. Only ten months after Rick's death, I gave the answer 'surviving' to someone I thought would understand. To my horror, she looked totally taken aback. I found it hard to believe that anyone could think I was doing anything more than surviving after so short a time. I never answered this question honestly again. It was a relief when someone asked me if I was keeping well, a question I could answer honestly.

A question I dreaded from meeting people I didn't know was whether I had children. I simply did not know how to answer it, so I avoided situations where I might have to enter into conversations that might lead to this question. I didn't want to say I had a son, which might lead on to further awkward questions, but neither did I want to deny him. I really wasn't happy just saying that I had a daughter, and it wasn't until 30th September 2018 that I had a breakthrough on this. I wrote in my journal, 'I've realised that Rick is in my heart and it is totally up to me what I reveal of what is in my heart. I have the choice who I reveal that to. I'm not denying Rick, just keeping him secret in my heart until the person, situation, or time is right, which may be never.' A thought added by Veronica was that Rick was too precious to talk about to people who he's not going to mean anything to. The choice was mine, and I at last felt comfortable about this question.

Some things also made me feel set apart, and one of these was the fact that people no longer shared things with me. Sometimes they would start to share, and then suddenly stop and say they shouldn't bother me with it as I was going through far worse. I found it very hurtful that people seemed to think I'd lost my ability to be interested in them, or to be concerned about them. Although I did feel that I had nothing to give, I was still capable of listening, and I actually found it helpful to focus on someone else's situation for a while. I always encouraged them to continue.

Most important to me, were those things that people said to me that were reassuring and encouraging. It helped so much to be told that the things I was thinking and feeling were normal, and I wasn't going mad. That I didn't need to feel guilty about the things I couldn't do, and I would be able to when I was ready. I needed this sort of reassurance a lot of times when I could not begin to see a way forward, or how anything could change. I knew I would never get over Rick's death, but I had to learn to live with it, and people's encouragement was vital in that process, and in giving me hope.

Chapter 8 - I can't take another step

The forest area had more boardwalks, and as I stepped off one of these, I turned my ankle. Without my walking pole I would have fallen over. For a short while, my ankle was too painful to take my weight, but gradually the pain subsided and I was able to hobble on. It felt fragile for the rest of the walk, but no worse than that. I only discovered the true extent of the injury, at the end of the walk, when I removed my walking boots. My ankle started to hurt again and became swollen. By the end of the day I could not put any weight on it at all. It made me wonder how I had managed to walk so far after injuring it.

Leaving the forest area, we found ourselves in the worst part yet. We had traversed a lot of bog, but nothing like this. There was no path, no posts, no boardwalks, no ways round, and it didn't smell very pleasant either. We just had to plough through as best we could, balancing on tussocks of grass or moss that we hoped would take our weight. Each step needed careful consideration as moss that looked solid, often wasn't. I was going more and more slowly, and David was leaving me behind. I finally got to the point where I couldn't take another step. I gave up and sat down on a log. I was totally exhausted and I knew that, if we ever got out of the bog, there was still a steep hill to climb and a ridge to walk along. I was convinced I couldn't make it. It was a good job that at this point I didn't know how tough the ridge was going to be! I don't have a big appetite, but I do need to eat regularly. I needed lunch, but lunch was in the car. A boiled fruit sweet and a drink of water helped, but it wasn't enough. I knew that I couldn't actually stay where I was, and the smell was starting to become too much. I was the only one who could do anything about it. So I forced myself to my feet, and began slowly and carefully to put one foot in front of the other.

Everything we had been through since Rick's death had taken its toll on me. It was on the 11th March 2016 that I recorded in my journal that I'd realised that I was running on empty. I had continued in this way until May 2017. There had been some top ups, but mostly it had been a continual drain on my resources. This was especially true of the operation, and the situations with David's parents and with Anna. This was not sustainable, and eventually I got to the point where I couldn't carry on anymore. I crashed physically, emotionally and mentally. I'd hit low points before, but this time I knew that this was definitely as far as I could go. I had got to the point where I couldn't take another step. Like my ankle before I took my boots off, I hadn't realised quite how badly injured I was.

On the 3rd May 2017 I wrote in my journal 'I feel I've come to the end and just can't cope anymore with demands being placed on me. I've nothing left to give and no strength. Can't see a way out and I feel beyond help.' I was in a very dark place and talking to Veronica, I totally fell apart. When David came home, she told him how I was feeling, and I was able to stop pretending to be all right when I wasn't. I needed to rest a lot as my body had crashed, and I was unable to do anything without feeling totally weak and exhausted. It was during one of these periods of rest that I realised, as I did on the walk, that I was the only one who could do anything about this. I knew that, as a result of the battering we had undergone over the last two plus years, I had not processed the bereavement in the way I needed to. Grieving had often had to be put on hold, while time and energy went into everything else. I was struggling to see a way forward, but God provided for me again.

As I previously mentioned, I'd turned my back on God after my operation, but he had not let go of me. I had felt as though I'd been knocked back too many times, and my faith hadn't meant much to me at that point. In some distant way I'd known that God was still with me, and four months after my operation I had randomly decided to go to the communion service. I had no idea why, and I hadn't expected to engage with the service, but I had. The verses read before the confession were Matthew 11:28-29, which were about being heavy laden and coming to be given rest. They had felt like an invitation God was giving to me at that point, and I can only describe what happened as something shifting within me, and I'd wanted to respond. In the weeks that followed, I still hadn't felt able to read the bible or pray, but I had kept going to church and had found it helpful just being there. I realise now it was all I was capable of at that time, and I'm sure God understood that.

I had continued in this way, just about holding on, until the second anniversary of Rick's death when a friend had given me a book, called 'Jesus Calling,'[1] and it was just what I'd needed. It had daily readings, which were a length I could manage and they had given me hope. They often included a description to illustrate something, and I'd found the pictures these created easy to hold on to. The bible references were just one verse, and I'd found I could focus on it as I didn't lose concentration in the way I did reading a passage. It had certainly drawn me back to God, and my journal from this time is full of quotes of extracts from the readings and verses that I'd found helpful. The result of this was that at the time I crashed I was seeking God, and in a place where I was receptive to what he was showing me.

So as I struggled to see a way forward, a bereavement retreat, which I had seen in the Scargill programme, came into my mind. I had been to

Scargill previously on a retreat and found it to be a very special place. Scargill House is in the Yorkshire Dales surrounded by beautiful scenery. I had felt close to God there and found healing. It was somewhere I felt safe. I discovered the retreat was only a week away. I wasn't sure how I was going to find the energy to drive there, or how I could cope with meeting new people, or sharing something that was so painful. However, the idea of Scargill just wouldn't go away, so eventually I gave in and booked a place. As on the walk, I had managed to get up from the log and take my first few slow steps forward.

When the day came to go, I wasn't at all sure I could drive that far. The only thing that made me attempt it was the conviction that God wanted me to go. I stepped out in faith and set off, and once I had, these words came into my mind, 'You concentrate on the driving and I'll do the rest.' I knew then that God would give me the strength I needed for the journey. I had left early to give myself plenty of time, and I was aiming to get to Grassington for lunch. I got to within 9 miles of Grassington before I felt I really needed to take a break, which was amazing. I easily achieved my aim, but I was tired and after lunch I fell asleep in the car. I woke up to the sound of birds singing. As I came round, at first I thought I was on the sofa in the lounge, but gradually realised I wasn't, and I really wanted to be! As I worked out where I was, I didn't want to open my eyes and find out I was right. I felt totally unable to carry through what I'd started. I spent a while trying to force myself to get out of the car to go and find a cup of tea. Then I had to force myself to finish the journey, and I only carried on because it was much too far to drive home again!

I felt better once I'd been welcomed at Scargill and shown to my room. It had three beds in it, and at first I felt I didn't want to be in a room that large. I was also faced with the problem of which bed to sleep in, decisions really were that difficult to make! Then I looked out of the window, and I knew why I had that room. There was a comfortable chair in front of a door to a small balcony with a view. Over the next few days, I spent quite a bit of time sitting in the chair watching the lambs, rabbits, and birds in the field. I could also see a garden area, and further away hills and woods. As I sat reflecting and processing I found it a calming place to be. The rest of the scenery around the house was stunning, and I knew this in my head, but somehow I couldn't feel it in the way I had on my first visit. Being untouched by this beauty, was one of the things that brought home to me what a bad place I was in.

There were eight people on the retreat and three leaders. On the first evening, we had to say the name of the person who had died and our relationship. I was the only one who had lost a child, and I felt singled out as a 'special case' needing extra support. This was done in a very loving way, but it was a shock that even in a group of bereaved people, I was seen as different. They were a lovely group of people, and I felt very included in the group in one way, but in another I felt isolated. Over the next few days, even with all they were going through, they all said in different ways they couldn't imagine going through the loss of a child.

The trouble was, I had been in partial denial about how awful it was to lose a child. I knew on one level it was devastating and tragic, but at the same time I had to convince myself I could survive. It was as if I couldn't accept the enormity of it in my head, even though I was actually feeling how bad it was. A friend had even said to me that my heart was broken, but my immediate reaction was to think, no, it's not as bad as that. To stop myself getting overwhelmed, I would think of people who were suffering far worse than me. That didn't take away what I was feeling, but somehow made it ever so slightly more manageable, and stopped me feeling sorry for myself. I also thought of the numbers of mothers who had lost sons through war, and reminded myself that a lot of people had been in my position before, and had survived it. As well as this, I was seeing David and others cope with the loss of a child, so I had to cope too, and to do that I wasn't facing facts. It took a group of bereaved people to help me to truly accept that it really was as bad as it gets.

On the next day we all told our stories. It was hard listening to what everyone had been through, but at the same time it was a relief to me to find that I could still feel for other people. The leaders handled everything very sensitively, so although it was painful to relive that time, it felt like a safe place to say it all, and to mention some of the things that had happened since. When we moved on to something creative, I really struggled. We were provided with magazines to create a collage about the person we had lost. I sat and aimlessly looked through the magazines. I managed to cut out two or three pictures, but I was really finding it hard to engage. I got totally stuck then one of the leaders suggested I wrote words instead of using pictures. With her prompting me I managed to think of things. It felt as though, with everything that had happened, Rick had been pushed into the background, and I was struggling to bring him back to the surface. It also showed how mentally exhausted I was.

I had not been sleeping well, and another bad night meant I wasn't in a good place at the start of the next day. I also didn't want to do what I knew was planned. We had been asked to take something that held special memories for us. I had taken the CD, which Rick had recorded for me, of him playing songs from Mission Praise on his keyboard. The memories were of the times we'd spent in his room with him playing his keyboard, and the way we'd shared together. They felt such precious memories that I didn't want to share them. Others volunteered to take a turn, but I couldn't do it until one of the leaders asked me directly if I would. It was better once I'd started, but I had to admit I couldn't listen to it and I shared about not coping with music. One of the leaders commented that it must be so silent in my heart at the minute, which really struck home as being true. This was another indication of the bad place I was in. It was suggested we should leave the things on the table for a while and I found it very hard to leave the CD there.

I had been looking forward to the relaxation session in the evening. I managed to relax, but then we had to imagine ourselves in a safe place. My mind flitted about, but couldn't settle on anything apart from walking along beside Rick and not being able see his face. I couldn't get rid of this picture, which was very upsetting, and I just sat there longing for the session to end. Again I felt that I'd pushed Rick too much into the background as I'd tried to cope with everything else. My times with Veronica had stopped me doing that completely, but I was scared that I might forget things about him and that some memories might be lost. When I talked to one of the leaders afterwards, she suggested that I should see my doctor, and get some help to lift my mood in order to be able to deal with some of the issues. She said she wasn't normally so directive. Coupled with the fact that Veronica had said the same, and she rarely told me what I should do, I accepted that I was going to have to go down this route.

A better night's sleep meant that I felt better the next day. We created memory jars, which involved using pastels to colour piles of salt, which was therapeutic in itself. We had to choose the colours to represent a memory of the person, and then layer them into a jar, and fix a tag with a colour code round the top. Again I needed help to complete this, I felt like a child that needed to be kept on task as I kept drifting off. In spite of that I found it a positive thing to do. Later we had a simple candle service, and the lighted candles were placed next to our memory jars. It was emotional, but very special.

There is a walled garden at Scargill and I wanted to go there, but hadn't been able to make myself, a further indication of the place I was in. Two of the group went after the service, so I asked if I could go with them. It was a wonderful place, and once we'd wandered round enjoying the flowers and plants I stayed there on my own. I sat on a bench and soaked up the atmosphere. It was so tranquil and the only sounds were the birds, the buzzing of the bees, and the breeze blowing through the trees. I felt very peaceful, and for that short space of time I found rest. I knew I'd found a safe place to return to in my head.

I enjoyed the community prayers in the chapel each morning. The words were so simple and meaningful, and were never rushed, with periods of silence. I was surprised at how I could feel the presence of God in the chapel when I was in such a low place, and it was an important part of my time there. On the last evening, we had a communion service in the chapel and again the words were lovely. The chaplain read a poem called, 'You have enough of me' by Ann Voskamp[2] and I felt as though God was speaking directly to me through the words. There was so much reassurance in hearing this:

You have enough of Me and courage
to do this hard thing.
You have enough of Me and strength

to not give up.
You have enough of Me and love
to keep on giving.
You have enough of Me and peace
to know that you are carried.
You have enough of Me
to simply rest.
You have enough of Me
and I am enough.
You are enough – because the great I AM
is in you...and with you...and for you.
And that alone is
completely enough.

We were invited to stay at the front, after we had taken communion, for a prayer for healing. I wasn't very clear what I wanted healing from, other than that I felt in a total mess. I decided to stay, and as the chaplain prayed for me the words 'broken heart' came very strongly into my mind. I went back to my seat wondering if God could heal a broken heart; to me it felt irreparable. The words that came into my mind then were that he binds up the broken hearted. I went back to my room and cried for a long time. This had brought me to the point where I fully acknowledged, and accepted, my brokenness. I think it was a point I needed to reach before healing could take place. As on the walk, the process of healing for my ankle could not begin until I had removed my boots, and the full extent of the injury became apparent. I was then able to begin the process with ice to bring the swelling down. I felt totally defeated, but God had prepared me for this with the words of the poem, and I clung on to the fact that he is enough.

We had also been given a poem called 'Broken pieces,' written by Helen Brocklehurst[3] from the Scargill Community, which was based on the Japanese art of mending pottery. The broken pieces are repaired with a special lacquer containing gold, silver, or platinum so that the repair is visible. The result of this is that the repaired pottery is similar, but different.

I thought I had it firmly in my grip
but then – that momentary slip
and now it lies there, shattered,
a thing that really mattered,
broken pieces, scattered
on the floor
and something that was precious is no more.

Desperately I scrabble around,
gather up the pieces from the ground
but as I try, despair increases –
I can't mend these broken pieces,
my futile effort ceases,
I'm not sure –
are they really precious anymore?
They'll never be the way they were before.

He takes each broken fragment, every shard,
the bits I would give up on and discard.
He makes them new yet recognised,
both familiar and disguised,

I'd never dreamed or realised
what he can do
with broken pieces, making something new.

This poem had become even more meaningful in the context of the realisation of my broken heart, and the fact that the rest of me felt as though it was in pieces too. By reaching this point I had painfully dragged myself to the end of the bog.

Chapter 9 - Firm ground

It was so good to get to the end of the bog and reach the track. I could not believe how wonderful it felt simply to be on firm ground. A wide, easy to follow track was in front of us. I felt better just for seeing the way forward, and being able to walk without watching every step. This lasted for a short way, but then the track went up the hill. The path was steep and rocky, which made it a hard climb as we tried to find the easiest way. We needed to stop for plenty of rests as we ascended. It did, however, feel as though progress was being made.

My time at Scargill, and my acceptance of the place I was in, had put me on firm ground. I knew that God was going to give me the strength for what was to come, and that the next stage of my journey through thick and thin was about healing. I knew too that the first step I needed to take was medication, so as with the track I could see a way forward. However, this soon led me to the foot of a hill, and I began a hard climb requiring lots of rest, and decisions to be made about the best way forward.

One of the first things I did was to look for verses referring to a broken heart. The words that had come into my mind about binding up the broken hearted were part of Isaiah 61:1. There were two further verses that were relevant:

'The Lord is close to the broken-hearted and saves those who are crushed in spirit.' Psalm 34:18

'He heals the broken-hearted and binds up their wounds.' Psalm 147:3

These were reassuring words as I began the steep climb.

The medication wasn't a quick fix, and I struggled for a while with the side effects. I was unable to see what else I could do as a way forward, and I felt very low and exhausted. My journal entries at this time reflected the fact that I was completely worn out, and I needed to take care of myself physically. I was sleeping quite a bit during the day, and dragging myself around the rest of the time. I tried to go for a walk each day to get some exercise, but it upset me to find how short a distance I could manage. I did have good days where I felt a bit stronger, but they were only occasional, and it was discouraging to go back into exhaustion the next day. Sometimes I accepted the need to rest, but at others I got frustrated with what I saw as a lack of progress. Patience has never been my strong point!

I was also aware that I needed to continue what had been started at Scargill, to focus on Rick and to continue to process the loss. The DVD of his wedding came up in conversation with Veronica, and we ended up watching it together. It was so lovely to see him moving around, and to be reminded of some of his mannerisms, and the way he spoke and laughed. At the same time it was so painful, and I longed to be able to touch him. It was very emotional, especially hearing the words 'till death us do part,' and the prayers for their future together, which was to be so short. There was part of me wanted to watch it over and over again, but another part of me couldn't face it. Although I was tearful for some days afterwards, it still felt like a positive thing to have done and a step forward.

In June we had the first of three holidays. These were all part of the healing process. We booked at the last minute, and I was very doubtful about my ability to cope with packing and the journey. Based on the weather forecast we decided to go to Lincolnshire, but it felt very stressful choosing the actual location and the self-catering cottage. David didn't seem to be any more decisive than I was. When we arrived at the cottage my heart sank. It was small, but perfectly adequate for the two of us, and it took me a while to realise what the problem was. I could reach to touch the ceilings, which meant they were very low indeed! I did get used to it though, and the lovely weather meant we didn't have to spend much time indoors. I loved the feeling of space that the countryside and beaches gave me. We did manage some walks, but they were short, and we spent quite a bit of time resting and enjoying the scenery. It was a respite, but I didn't want to go back home, and I didn't feel in a much better place as a result of that holiday.

Anna had been told she would be leaving the unit at the end of June. The time of the birthdays was one she found particularly hard, so it was a really bad point for this to happen. She didn't want to come back home, and we didn't feel it was right for her to do so. It hadn't worked before, so we needed to try something different. She was given no guidance or support in finding somewhere to live. Even worse was that, nobody seemed to be doing anything to put in place any care in the community. While we were away, she managed to find a room in a house with two others to rent. I was very unsure if she was ready for this, and the fear of what might happen was hanging over us. Going from 24/7 care to nothing was a huge jump.

A visit to the GP put bereavement counselling back in the picture again as a way forward. I still didn't want to do it, but was more willing to look into it. She gave me a number to ring, which I did and was told I would have to wait three weeks for a telephone assessment. In the meantime, I was sent a form to fill in as preparation. I went into panic mode when I read the form, not a good start! It felt very intrusive, and I didn't want to answer the questions never mind talk to a clinician about them. I felt so stressed by it until I read Psalm 62:6, 'Truly he is my rock and my salvation; he is my fortress, I shall not be shaken.' I was aware of a calm coming over me as I realised I didn't need to be shaken by this. It did, however, make me question whether it was the right way to be going.

I spent a long time on this question. At Veronica's suggestion, I spoke to a lovely lady from the Diocesan counselling service who gave me more idea of what to expect. It would involve reflecting on and exploring where I am and the issues, making sense of the journey, and giving insight so that I could find my own way forward and answers for myself. I could see how it could help. We then talked about the importance of being ready to do it, and that if I was feeling it as a pressure I maybe wasn't ready. She said counselling was not an easy option. Well, I was very aware of that! There were no easy options.

I began to wonder if it was possible to find a different way forward. When I first crashed in May I was totally worn out. I was withdrawing as a way of coping, and there were lots of things I couldn't do, but I couldn't really explain why I couldn't do them. There was just a block which prevented me. The assessment form had shown me that I was in a really bad place, and it had scared me. However, I was improving physically as I was having runs of several better days, and my energy levels were increasing. Maybe I just needed time and space to recover physically, and then other things would become manageable again. All this questioning was actually a distraction from working through the loss. In my journal on the 9th July I wrote, 'Maybe this just can't be rushed and people are trying to fix me in too much of a hurry. I'm going round in circles and I'm tired of thinking about it.'

At the same time as questioning this, I had to cope with the birthdays and concern for Anna. Her care co-ordinator rang to ask what our concerns were. Well, where was I to start with that one! I was unprepared for the call, but managed to think of several concerns without much effort. We eventually heard, at the last moment, that she would not be discharged until a care plan was in place. We then went to the opposite extreme. Anna was allowed time out to stay at a friend's house to look after their cats while they were away. The psychiatrist decided he wanted her to make the ninety minute drive back to the unit after a few days, so they could assess how she was doing. It was the inconsistency I was struggling to cope with. One minute she was to leave without support, and the next she wasn't expected to cope for a week, it didn't make sense. We all felt it was unreasonable, so that involved me in another long phone call to try and sort it out. I felt very stressed by this. I was concerned that if she really did need that support, then I was putting her at risk by complaining about it. They changed their minds and all went smoothly, but I had totally lost confidence in the unit. I was feeling overwhelmed again, and none of it had been about Rick.

I eventually managed to fill in the assessment form, and I felt very calm before the phone call. The clinician couldn't have been nicer. After I'd given him the answers from the form, he made me feel it was understandable to be as I am, given the circumstances. I found it reassuring to be told that by someone who was regularly doing these assessments. I was to be referred to a counsellor, but I would have to wait three or four months. In the meantime, I needed to look after myself, and work towards doing the things that gave me a sense of achievement. I was very happy about this outcome as it took the pressure off. It gave me space to get stronger, and to see what ways forward I could find on my own.

The day after this, we left for our second holiday, this time in Cumbria. We had another week of good weather, the scenery was stunning, and we did a lot of walking. I was able to manage so much more than I had in Lincolnshire, and it was encouraging to find out how much I had improved. It was often quiet and peaceful on our walks, and I could feel this, and the beauty of creation, doing me good. For the first time in ages, I was experiencing enjoyment. I felt better for this holiday, but then I panicked that the physical improvement meant I should be able to do more. As we packed to come home and I couldn't work out where to start, or make simple decisions, I realised I still had a long way to go. When we got home, I also found that I was still unable to go out by myself. The holidays were just part of the recovery process, and change was slow.

Anna was finally discharged at this point with no care plan, but a care co-ordinator who was going to see what he could sort out for her. We were obviously concerned about this. She adapted very quickly, however, and settled into her new life. After six months she rented a flat by herself. We have been impressed with the level of care in the community that has been available to her. With this support she continued to cope, although life at times was a struggle for her.

I tried not to focus on the things I couldn't do, or be discouraged by them. Sometimes I succeeded in this, at other times I didn't. I knew it was important to find areas where I could make progress. Along with the assessment form, I'd been sent some notes, which included helpful things to do on your own. Some of these seemed possible for me to attempt. One was to write about the person you had lost, and your life together as a family. I knew this would be hard, but I felt that to engage with the memories was something I needed to do. I had also wanted to sort out and print photos I had on the computer, and it seemed like the right time to do this as part of the process. The notes also suggested reading about other people's experience. This was something I'd avoided as being too painful, and a trigger. They were positive ways forward, but I knew I would need Veronica's support in this, which she was very willing to give.

One of the first things I did was to see if there were any CDs at church with Rick's sermons on. The services were recorded each week, but I didn't know how long the CDs were kept for, and it suddenly became very important to me to have any that were there. It was so thrilling to take the top one off a stack to find the next one had Rick Cole written on it. I felt as if I'd found something very precious. We found two more, but there were none before 2012. At that point I wasn't sure if I'd be able to listen to them, but it was lovely to have them.

A friend had come across a book written by a mother who had lost her son. As she told me about it, I realised the author was someone who had come to our church a while ago to talk about her experience, so I was already familiar with her story. My friend offered to get it for me, and rather hesitantly I agreed. The book, by Philippa Skinner, was called 'See you soon,' and I found the title, and the picture on the front cover of her son leaving, heart rending before I'd even opened it. In the introduction, she wrote about signposts to finding the way through, which had been left by others who had walked similar ways in the 'dark and devastating world of child loss.'[1] I knew I was going to find it hard to read her book, and that there would be triggers for me, but I was encouraged by the idea of finding signposts.

It took me a while, and it was a very moving book to read, but I slowly made my way through it. Our circumstances were very different, but I could relate to a lot of what she said, and I found it very helpful in validating my feelings. The most positive signpost for me was the concept of continuing bonds. I was very excited to read this sentence, 'Our relationship with the person we loved while they were alive carries on in a changed form after death.'[2] My experience had been that in the anguish that followed finding out that Rick had died, I felt my relationship with him had ended, and that the emotional bonds had been cruelly severed. He had been torn away from me, and there was a huge gap between us. The possibility that I could maintain my relationship with Rick, albeit in a different way, was so life giving.

I wanted to find out all I could about this possibility, and Veronica leant me a book on continuing bonds. I did gain greater understanding, but in my befuddled state my brain was struggling to cope with it all. It didn't matter as the basics had really struck a chord with me. As I reflected on those things that made me feel connected to Rick, I enthusiastically began to think about what my ways of maintaining the bonds would be. I could see that without realising it, I had already been making some connections. An obvious one being the children's talk at church, and another was wearing his ring on a chain round my neck at Christmas. Finding more connections, and maintaining my relationship with Rick, developed over time and was a very special way forward for me. It felt very personal, very creative, and very positive.

One of the connections I had was the CDs of his sermons, so I eventually plucked up the courage to listen to one with Veronica. This also included the children's talk, and as his theme was worship he talked about one of the songs we sang at the holiday club. He then got everyone to sing it with the actions. There were so many memories wrapped up in that, and I really struggled to listen to it. The sermon was easier until he talked about God showing him the way he wanted him to go in the future. That really got to me and brought back the pain of the senselessness and waste. Hearing his voice evoked a sense of loss, which was overwhelming. I wanted the sermon to carry on, but at the same time I wanted it to stop. In spite of that, I felt that listening to him speaking at church was something I was grateful to be able to do.

Another connection was the CD of him playing the keyboard, which I'd taken to Scargill. I tried to listen to it, but the pain was too much and that quickly went off. Although there were positive memories attached to it, they were more than I could bear at that moment. I could still only do what I was ready for. I also looked on the website of Rick's placement church, when he was a student, to see if there were any of his sermons. I found one and then emailed them to see if they had any more. They kindly sent me six, and again it was so special to have them. Sometimes, when I was with Veronica, I felt strong enough to listen to one, at other times I couldn't face it. It was very painful, but it was part of him that I still had.

I also made connections with Rick in smaller ways. One simple way was when we played a game, which in itself was a connection with Rick; I chose to play with the colour that I knew he would have chosen. It became a comfort to find these connections, whereas in the past I'd avoided them as painful triggers. I had used avoidance a lot, partly because of all the other things I was coping with, but I decided it was time to stop doing that as far as I was able. This included going to church on a Sunday. Our friends, who worked in Uganda, were speaking about their work in an evening service. This was an incentive to go back to that church, for the first time for sixteen months. It made me aware of how much I'd missed the people, and I decided this was a loss I could do something about, so I pushed myself to go back to the morning services.

Our third holiday was in Northumberland. My brother had offered us their house for a week, in return for looking after their cat while they were away. For the third time, we had lovely weather and I fell in love with the area. Apart from the scenery, the beaches, the lovely light, and feeling of space, it was a special place to be. I was very comfortable there and felt at home. As I paddled in the sea, I thought that doing that was a link with Rick, but I felt very aware of his absence beside me. The words from a canticle came very strongly into my mind, 'Christ beside me on my left and my right.'[3] At first I didn't understand because nobody could fill Rick's space. Then I realised that Jesus had always been there, and he was still there even though Rick wasn't. It was comforting to be reminded of that. It was on this holiday that we did the walk described in this book. The fact that I did manage to complete this walk, with all its difficulties, showed me how much stronger I was physically. This holiday did me a lot of good.

Having recovered my strength, I was better able to tackle other areas. I'd decided that I would record my memories of Rick in a scrapbook, so that they could be random, and I wouldn't feel the need to get things in the right order. So I bought the scrapbook. As I'd found Philippa Skinner's book so helpful, I also decided to read more books for bereaved parents. I based my choice on the reviews and ordered three books. These both seemed positive ways forward, and along with listening to the CDs, and the discovery of continuing bonds, I felt ready to move on. I had reached the top of the hill, but forward progress was not going to be easy. There was a lot of hard work ahead.

Chapter 10 - Along the ridge

W e had reached the top of the hill, but there was still further to go. We stopped to catch our breath and look at the view, which was spectacular, but I was not able to fully appreciate it. I was trying to summon up the energy to walk along the ridge. I had assumed that walking along the top of the ridge would be flat, but of course it wasn't. That would have been too easy! Instead, we were faced with a steep descent, followed by a steep climb back up again, along a rocky path. At the top of each hill, we realised that we had got to repeat the process again, then again and again, with no concept of how near we were to the end.

This reflects the next stage of my journey, which was far from flat. I alternated between going down, and dragging myself back up again, as I tried to make progress. I never went as far down as the bottom of the steep hill I had climbed to reach the top of the ridge. However, I had some difficult times as I tried to work through and process things. I continued to go up and down physically, emotionally, mentally, and spiritually. I was still experiencing times of exhaustion and dragging myself through each day. At times I felt emotionally dead, and at other times I was overwhelmed by grief, which left me with it very near the surface. Motivation and concentration were still a struggle, and I often felt very low. It didn't take much to throw me, or put me on overload. I sometimes found that I drew closer to God, but at other times I was keeping him at a distance. It often felt there was no end in sight, and I struggled to keep going, but there were positive things that helped me to get to the top of the next hill.

Shortly after returning from holiday, I eventually started to be able to go out by myself. My first attempt was in the pouring rain! I thought that not many other people would be stupid enough to go out, and I could hide under my umbrella! Although I still didn't feel comfortable, I continued to push myself to do this. I also started driving again, which meant I was also able to go back to the midweek communion service. I hadn't been for five months, since I'd crashed in May, and I had missed it. For a while, I sometimes managed to go to church on a Sunday. The church had a new pastor, and I found his sermons helpful and encouraging. He was honest, and he was real about life and how that affects our faith. So even his challenges contained an acknowledgement that not everyone would be in a place to face that challenge, at that point in time, and that was acceptable. Statements like, 'if you got to church even though it was an effort then good on you' were uplifting for me, and helped me to feel included even though I wasn't in a good place. I still struggled with some of the songs and had to go out if it got too much.

I was further challenged when a friend told me she was taking over the children's group, which I'd run in the past, and asked if I would like to help. My initial reaction was that I would love to, and I felt quite excited about it, especially as children's work was a link with Rick. At four o'clock in the morning, however, it did not seem such a good idea! It meant a weekly commitment, when I would have to go out and be with people, no matter how I was feeling. I decided I would do it if I was really needed. I found that I was, so I had to step out in faith that God would help me each week. My friend was sensitive to where I was, and she understood that I didn't want any responsibility, so I felt safe with her. I found it very hard to go each week, but once I got on with it, I knew God was strengthening me. There were some good moments, but on the whole I felt I was just muddling through, and I was glad when it was over for another week.

I also started on the scrapbook fairly soon after the holiday, and this proved to be a very up and down process. On the title page I put the heading, 'Memories of Rick,' and then added a picture of him as a baby, and a recent one. I got very upset typing the dates of his life; I felt he really shouldn't have an end date yet. I wasn't sure how I was going to continue with it. Being caught out by the title page was totally unexpected, and I couldn't see how I was going to cope with the rest of it. However, I managed to push myself to carry on, and on the next few pages I wrote words that described Rick, the things he had a heart for, my relationship with him, and the thing we enjoyed doing together. I had been thinking about it for a while, and it was good to get my thoughts down on paper. It felt like a very positive thing to be doing.

I sorted out photos I had taken of Rick, which caused some tearful moments, but at other times I felt more detached as I concentrated on completing the task. It evoked a lot of memories as I tried to put them in date order. Someone from church regularly took photos at any event we held, so I asked if she could give me any photos of Rick. I realised it wasn't going to be easy for her as she must have thousands of photos. She kindly found some and put them on a disc for me, and again I felt I was being given something very precious. I eventually managed to decide which photos to have printed, both for the scrapbook and to go in albums.

I made a list of memories I wanted to include in the scrapbook, which I was constantly adding to. I gradually worked through this list, as I randomly selected memories to write about, and photos to stick in. Some days I found it helped to do it, but I had other days when I simply couldn't face it. I always had to push myself to start, but I had to learn to recognise those times when it would have done me more harm than good to carry on. Sometimes I felt all right while I was working on it, but then I found it hard to adjust back to the present. That was when it hit me the most. I found it very draining. However, it felt good to be recording these memories, and to engage with them in this way. Even when the memories triggered grief and were painful, I could see that they were a positive thing, and they held the potential of becoming even more so in the future.

However, not all the memories were good ones, and these became an issue for me. As I thought about whether I could have done more for Rick through the difficult points in his life, I found myself struggling with a sense of guilt. This was definitely a time of going down for me. Veronica helped me to have a different perspective on it. She thought that we wouldn't have had such a good relationship if he'd blamed me at all. I thought of things he'd said and written to me which backed this up, but the guilt was still there.

I'd been reading one of the books about surviving the loss a child by Gary Roe, which had the very apt title, 'Shattered.' I found the chapter on guilt helpful, including the following suggestion, 'Write a letter or poem to your child expressing the guilt you feel. Be as specific as you can.'[1] It was a while before I could face doing it, and it proved very emotional. It then took me some time before I could follow the rest of his suggestions. Eventually I was able to read the letter out loud, imagining Rick was there. I asked for his forgiveness, God's forgiveness, and then wrote, 'I forgive myself' at the bottom, and said it out loud.[2] Then I took it further by laying the burden of guilt at the foot of the cross. Finally I shredded the letter. I knew that I would have got things wrong, but I had dealt with the issue as far as I could and I felt lighter.

I found reading the books for bereaved parents hard and challenging, but they were definitely a positive during this time. As well as the chapter on guilt, I found the rest of 'Shattered' to be the most helpful. It had short, easy to read chapters, which had practical suggestions at the end, and it affirmed that all I was experiencing emotionally, mentally, physically, spiritually, and relationally was natural. I found reassurance in this, and I was also relieved to find that because we will be different, we may not recognise ourselves. He writes, 'This identity crisis is a natural and common experience for those suffering the loss of a child.'[3] I had no idea who I was anymore, but it was encouraging to read that this identity crisis should only be temporary, 'As we process the grief, we will adapt, adjust, heal and grow (though any and all of these might seem impossible on any given day). But we will not go back to who we were. That's impossible.'[4] All the books I read provided comfort and encouragement in the fact that the things I was working through had been experienced by others in a similar situation. It was also helpful to read about how others had overcome things, and how they had learnt to manage certain situations.

One of the concepts that I had to think through, as a result of what I'd read, was that of living in a way that honours your child and their memory. I didn't feel that should be the motivation for what I did, but I did want to honour Rick. As I processed this, I thought that Rick had wanted to follow God's will for his life, and I knew he would want me to do the same. It's what God wants too, so I decided that if I'm doing what God wants then I'm honouring Rick at the same time. Having worked through this, when I listened to one of Rick's sermons he spoke about doing what God has called us to do, which confirmed my thoughts. More than once, when I listened to Rick's sermons, they contained something relevant to what I'd been working through at that time.

Five months after making the initial phone call for bereavement counselling, I received a call offering me an appointment, the following week, with a bereavement counsellor. It took me by surprise as I'd almost forgotten about it. I knew that I was in a better place than when I had initially filled in the assessment form. As a result I felt I was making progress on my own, with Veronica's support, so I turned it down. I panicked a bit after I'd made this decision on the spur of the moment, but I'd never really wanted to have to do it in the first place. I also felt I needed longer to continue with the things I had started, which were proving to be helpful, before I went down that route if it proved necessary.

I needed space to work on the scrapbook, to read the books, and to process. It was important to me to know that I wouldn't be disturbed, so I usually did it while David was at work. He had been talking about retiring for quite some time, but had never done anything about it. Suddenly it became a reality as a replacement was found for him and he only had a few weeks left to go. This put me under pressure to try to finish the scrapbook, and reading the books, before I lost this space. It felt vital to me to have this space, and I wasn't sure how I would cope when it was gone. I tried to rush things that I really needed to take my time over. The result of this was that I often felt overwhelmed by it all. David eventually retired in December 2017. As I'd expected, I found it very hard when I did lose my uninterrupted space, and it took me a very long time to adjust to it. It was frustrating, but I did learn to use the short periods of space available to me, and I did eventually come to the end of all the things I'd thought to include in the scrapbook. I then only occasionally added to it as fresh things came to mind. Although hard, the scrapbook was overall a positive thing to have done and a definite way forward for me.

I had continued with my GP's suggestion of gardening when I felt able, and this had proved positive, even though the amount that needed doing had been daunting. During this time, I used it as a way of giving myself a break from the feelings brought to the surface by the scrapbook. Gardening was not about growing things, but about getting rid of things that shouldn't be there, and making things tidy. I put down black plastic on the vegetable patch, which we weren't using, to try to prevent the weeds and moss coming back. It was very much about bringing everything back under control, and keeping it that way. While so much of my life felt out of control, it became important to have control over something. Unfortunately, in a garden, this is a never ending process!

Another positive thing was drawing closer to God through a Quiet Day at the Anglican Church. I was unsure about going, and I couldn't make myself go in the morning. Then at lunchtime I suddenly decided I would go, because unless I tried I wouldn't know if a Quiet Day was something I would find helpful. I was immediately struck by the atmosphere as I walked into the church, and it felt like a safe place to be. It was my first experience of spending any length of time in silence and I loved it. The theme was the four seasons, and I found Veronica's reflections on each one, and the objects she gave us, a good place from which to start my own processing as I waited on God to see what he wanted to show me. I never would have thought God could show me so much through a ball of string, and a person shaped biscuit cutter! There were points too where I stopped processing, and it was lovely to just be, and to sense the presence of God. It was a very special day, and I came away feeling so much better for it.

After the Quiet Day, as so often happens when God is trying to grab our attention, I got the same message several times over. He was challenging me in various ways about spending time with him, including through one of Rick's sermons about spending time in the presence of God, and the need to be intentional about it. I started to explore different ways of doing this, and looking for a new way forward spiritually that was a fit for me. As the number of people attending the Sunday morning services grew over time, I started to become overwhelmed by how crowded and busy it was. I found that the noise level before the service started had become almost more than I could cope with. I knew then that it was no longer somewhere I could be, and I felt free to leave and to go to the Anglican Church. Although I felt a loss at leaving the people, I had changed and I needed to be part of a different sort of church.

However, I did continue to listen to some of the pastor's sermons on line. One of these was on our inner world, and was very relevant as it was about the new identity we have in Christ, which is vital. This identity never changes, even through the changes in life we all face. It struck me that this was something I hadn't lost, and it gave me a firm foundation as I questioned who I was, and who I was to become. I could no longer work out what I wanted to do, or felt able to do, what abilities I had, how I related to others, even what I did or didn't like. Parts of me, such as any sort of creativity, felt like they had died. I no longer had any passion for anything. It felt as though everything about me had been crushed. So part of my journey became about going to God for healing whilst learning about, and adapting to, the changes that had been wrought in me. The picture of a mosaic, in which something lovely is created from broken pieces, was important to me as I worked through this. I realised that although so much had just happened to me, and was out of my control, I did still have choices. With God's help I could make choices about who I became, so I could focus on positive responses rather than negative ones, and therefore avoid things like bitterness creeping in. This was a tough journey of discovery and it took time to work through. It sent me down, but became a way up as I made slow progress.

One of the things that came out of this was the realisation that I was feeling angry with God because of all that had happened. As a result of this, I was fluctuating between seeking God, and not wanting to have anything to do with him. Veronica leant me a book containing the Authorised Version of the Psalms. I spent some time dipping into the Psalms and reflecting on the random way in which they change subject and mood. They express so much, as the Psalmist doesn't hold back on his feelings. I decided that a way to deal with the anger was to write in the style of the psalms, expressing this and other feelings and thoughts too, both negative and positive. Once I started it just flowed, and I went to a lot of places I hadn't expected to. It felt a very positive and freeing thing to have done.

I also realised that I was feeling guilty about what happened at the time of Rick's death, and I couldn't make decisions because I didn't trust my judgement anymore. Although I'd realised he was very unwell when I rang on the Thursday, I felt guilty that I hadn't fully recognised how bad he was. I'd believed the doctor who'd said he would be better by Monday, so I hadn't rung the next day to find out how he was. My focus had been elsewhere, and I'd made the decision that I didn't need to worry about him on top of everything else. By Saturday it was too late. I felt that I hadn't cared enough for him at that point in his life, and it seemed as though he had died while my back was turned. I felt as though, in spite of what I had learned about continuing bonds, I had been responsible for severing the bond between us by the decisions I had made. This sent me spiralling down, and it was a while before I could make any progress with this. I wrote him another letter, and I also came to the conclusion that Rick would have understood why I'd made the decisions I had, and he would have forgiven me. I also handed the burden of this over to God. It wasn't until months later that I was finally able to fully deal with this, although I will always wish I had done things differently.

Veronica was very reassuring that I had not severed the bond with Rick, and she suggested that a way of continuing my relationship with him was to write to him. I'd come across this in the books I'd read, but I'd thought it wasn't for me. I had written letters to him on specific things, but I wasn't sure I wanted to do more than that. She gave me a notebook to get me started, so I had no excuse! I felt better about the idea when I realised I could keep it private by writing in shorthand, so I decided to give it a go. I found it surprisingly helpful, and much easier to do than I'd thought it would be. I could write to him about things that had happened, how I felt about him, and about our relationship. It usually triggered grief, but it helped to do it, and to think what his response might be. I didn't do it often, but every now and again I felt the need to write to him about something, especially on tree stump days.

As before, whilst working through all this, I was also brought down by the extra stresses that everyday life can throw at you. One of these was David's health. He was experiencing pain, which led to him having to undergo various tests. We were back to waiting for the next test and then the results. This was hanging over us for ten months until he got a diagnosis, and then the correct level of medication. Arranging a weekend away for the wider family, for my mother's 90th birthday was stressful too, and I wasn't at all sure how I was going to cope with it. It proved to be bittersweet for me. It was a special time and it was lovely to be with everyone, but towards the end missing Rick began to get too much for me. Doing something that he had been part of in the past intensified the loss, and it was so painful.

Another stress was one which we brought on ourselves in some ways. We were exploring the idea of moving! We had always planned to move down south when David retired. I had got to the point where I wanted to leave the north and downsize years before. Rick knew how much I wanted to move, and he wanted it for me. We had thought it would be to Dorset. He wanted us close enough to be helpful, but far enough away not to be a nuisance! I understood what he meant, it was important we had our own lives, but we could be there for each other. On our visits to see Helen we had started to explore the area. After a while I realised that much as I loved the area, I could no longer move there as there were too many memories. We turned our attention to Sussex, so we could be near to my mother. On our visits there we did further exploration as we tried to narrow it down. We eventually settled on a town next to where I was brought up. It had felt a long process just to get this far, and hard to make decisions, or feel enthusiastic about anywhere.

As a result of David's retirement the prospect of moving became a reality. Part of me was desperate to move away and make a fresh start. Another part of me was very apprehensive about how I would cope with moving and starting a new life. I fluctuated between the two; I found it especially hard to think of leaving some very special friends. There was a lot of decorating and cleaning to be done to a rather neglected house to get it ready to go on the market, which we finally achieved in April 2018. In spite of the fact that this part of my journey through thick and thin was very up and down, progress was being made with God's help.

Chapter 11 - Where is the path?

Going up and down along the ridge, with no concept of what progress was being made, I was continually questioning how much further we had to go, and whether I had the strength left to make it. In fact, from the point where everything changed on the walk and it became so difficult, I was constantly asking questions. Some of these questions I couldn't find answers to at the time I was asking them, for others I only found partial answers. That didn't stop me asking them. A constant question on the walk was, 'where is the path?' We would find a partial answer to this, only to shortly find ourselves needing to ask the same question again! Others included: Are we going the right way? Why is it taking so long? Can we find a way out of this bog? Why is this so different from what we were expecting? Why did we leave our lunch in the car? Why does it seem so much further than we thought it would be?

So too, on top of everything else we were dealing with, there were many questions as a result of Rick's death. My first journal entry in March is full of them. Some questions were there from the beginning, whilst others took longer to surface, but were no less powerful in their intensity and the need for an answer. The main question that was there from the very beginning was the anguished cry of 'Why?' It was a constant question which burst forth out of the pain and the grief. It had to be expressed even though I knew there would not be an answer. Further specific questions were gradually added to the single 'why?'

Rick was a young man with so much potential, and he had so many ideas of how he might serve God in the future. He was loved by so many people who, according to things written or said about him, recognised his gifts, and valued the sort of person he was. He had touched so many lives, and he felt called into full time ministry. Are there really so many young people answering a call to train to be a pastor of a church that we can afford to lose one? My expectation was that God would use Rick even more in the future than he was at present. God does not promise that just because we are following his will things will go well. In fact in John 16:33 Jesus does the opposite and warns that, 'In this world you will have trouble.' So I never expected it to be easy for Rick, but I did expect that he would live that life. Why did he die at the age of 24? Why did God not heal him? His death simply did not make sense.

At his baptism at the age of 16, he had said that he had decided to go all out for God. So why did he only have 8 years in which to do that? Rick and Helen had a canvas in their lounge from their wedding service picturing them listening to the address. Underneath the picture were the words they had been challenged with from the wedding at Cana, 'Do whatever he tells you' (John 2:5). Why did they only have just under a year to do that together? Why was his life so short when he had so much potential, so much to give, and the willingness to give it?

How could he be rejoicing in heaven when he had left so much devastation behind? Rick was not like that, he hurt for other people. He would have been devastated at leaving Helen, and greatly distressed by the pain and grief his death was causing his family and friends. I wanted him to be safe, happy and rejoicing with the Lord, but I did not understand how he could be. It did not make sense to me. These were some of my questions about what had happened to Rick.

I also had other more general questions. How do you carry on when nothing makes sense anymore? It takes trust and faith to a whole new level. What does it actually mean to trust God on a daily basis? Where was God? How do I pray for other people and situations? Is God in control? These questions and more would keep repeating themselves. I knew it was all right to ask these questions. Following God through thick and thin does not mean that we shut our minds down. Life continually throws up questions, and we need to think through what we believe, and what our faith means in our daily walk with God. God knows that these questions are very real, especially in times of tragedy, and he wants us to be honest with him and to express them. The psalms are full of questions, and the prophets too voiced their questions and perplexities to God.

Right at the beginning, when the minister said that God's perspective is not the same as ours, at the back of my mind was the thought that this was probably as much of an answer as I was going to get. However, this did not stop me asking the questions, or trying to find some sort of answers, and it was right for me to do so. The process of searching for answers was painfully slow. When you are battling with motivation, the inability to concentrate, and when your mind constantly feels on overload, it is virtually impossible to read and to think through some of these big questions. I would begin a book I thought might help, but would then lose interest. At other times I simply could not take what I was reading. I do not recall actually throwing a book across the room, but I came close to it when I could not cope with the views being expressed. It would often be a while before I could engage with a book again, by which time I had lost the thread of the argument. I still persisted when I could. I knew I was not going to get answers to my often repeated 'why' questions, but there were other questions that needed to be explored.

I did not lose my faith, but I was no longer sure of what it meant in practice, what it meant to trust. One of the chapters from Shattered was on spiritual confusion and it concluded, 'Our normal view of the world can be rattled, torn or completely dismantled by this traumatic loss. Spiritual confusion and questioning during this time are natural and common.'[1] Dr James Dobson, in his book When God Doesn't Make Sense writes, 'Interestingly enough, pain and suffering do not cause the greatest damage. Confusion is the factor that shreds one's faith.'[2] I began to try to focus on those things I was sure about; God's love, Jesus' death on the cross so that we could be forgiven and reconciled with God, Jesus' resurrection and the certainty of eternal life for those who believe. The communion service encapsulated those things I felt had not changed. I also knew that God himself had not changed. It seemed important that I was asking questions in the context of those things of which I was sure.

One of my questions was answered on what would have been Rick's 25th birthday. We went for a walk in the Peak District, which was a walk Rick had always enjoyed. It was a hot day, and I kept thinking that it was so wrong that he was not enjoying this lovely weather on his birthday. We sat in the shade of a rock for a while, looking out over the lovely view. As I started thinking again about how Rick could possibly be rejoicing in heaven when he had left so much pain behind, I became overwhelmed by the need to know that he was all right. The words that came into my head were 'He's with me, why wouldn't he be?' At first I thought it was just what I wanted to hear, but this was followed with the words 'I have always been able to look after him better than you.' This was a well-deserved reprimand, but at the same time it was the reassurance I needed, and I felt a tremendous sense of peace moving through me. It was as if a burden had been lifted. God had graciously answered a question I should not really have needed to ask in the first place. He understood my need as a mother to know that my child was all right, and he responded to it. I also accepted that the answer to how he was all right, while we were not, was something we could not understand until we got to heaven ourselves.

However, other questions took more work, and then the answers were only partial and did not totally satisfy. The answers, such as they were, were often things I already knew, but I needed to be reminded of them and examine them again, in the light of what had happened. These questions included the difficult subject of suffering. Why does a God of love allow the evil, the suffering, and the tragedies, which are so prevalent, and which everyone is affected by at some time in their lives? Why do bad things happen to good people and some suffer far more than others? Why is life so unfair? A partial answer to this is that we live in a fallen world. Ever since Adam and Eve chose to disobey God, there have been repercussions for the whole of creation. Sin and death entered the world that God had created, bringing with them tragedies and suffering. None of us are immune to bad things happening, neither good people nor bad people, and it does appear to be random and unfair. This answer may be of small comfort, but nonetheless it is true that the fall affects us all, and this has to be taken into account in any discussion on suffering.

What we must also remember; is that God has involved himself in human suffering through Jesus' death on the cross. He did not distance himself from the world after the fall; he even went as far as becoming part of it. In writing about the cross as a revelation of love John Stott says, 'For the God who allows us to suffer once suffered himself in Jesus Christ, and he continues to suffer with us today. There is still a question mark against human suffering, but over that mark we boldly stamp another mark – the cross.'[3] I found this to be a strong image, and I drew a large question mark with a cross over the top. Looking at this drawing gave me an important perspective on this difficult question.

When things happen which do not make sense, it can lead us to question whether or not God is in control. This is a far-reaching question, and I have only scratched the surface of it.[4] The biblical evidence is that God is in control, even though this may not have been apparent to the people at the time. The Old Testament shows God working his purposes out through Israel's history, beginning with Abraham through to the return from exile. In the New Testament God's purposes are further seen in the life and death of Jesus.

The story of Joseph is an obvious example of God's control on a personal level. However, it did not appear that this was the case when Joseph was sold by his brothers into slavery, and then imprisoned for something he had not done. What was God doing? Joseph discovered, in spite of what had happened, that God was with him and made him successful, in both of those difficult situations. Eventually Joseph was released from prison, due to his God given ability to interpret dreams. He was then placed in charge of Egypt, under Pharaoh, to manage the years of abundance, and then the years of famine, which had been revealed in Pharaoh's dreams. When his brothers came to Egypt, to buy food because of the famine, Joseph was able to say to them, 'So then, it was not you who sent me here, but God' (Gen 45:8). He could look back to see how God had been working through all the dark times, to bring him to the point where he could save lives, including those of his family.

On a national level, the prophet Habakkuk questioned God about the violence and injustice he was seeing all around him in Judah. He wanted to know why God was doing nothing about it. God gave him an answer, but it was most certainly not one he was expecting, and was definitely not one he could understand. God was going to send the Babylonians to sort Judah out. The Babylonians are described as a ruthless, impetuous, feared, and dreaded people who are a law to themselves (Hab 1:6-7). The answer was shocking, but it did show Habakkuk that God was in control. He was at work even though Habakkuk had not been aware of the wider picture.

In the Gospels many did not understand Jesus' teaching and drifted away. When Jesus asked the disciples if they also wanted to leave, Peter answered, 'Lord, to whom shall we go? You have the words of eternal life. We believe and know that you are the Holy One of God' (John 6:68-69). In spite of this acknowledgement, they did not understand all he was telling them, and were left in complete bewilderment following his death. It is hard to imagine how devastating that must have been for them. At first they hardly dared to believe in the resurrection, but then they gradually came to understand the purposes of God through these events. The rest of the New Testament shows that although the early Christians faced many difficulties and trials, God was in control of the spread of the gospel message.

It is easier for us, with an overview of all that was happening at that time, to see God in control. For the people involved at the time, however, it was no easier for them, than it is for us now, to see and understand what God was doing. Having realised that God was in control of the nations, Habakkuk then went on to question God's solution to the problem. The Babylonian nation was far worse than Judah, so it did not make sense that God would use them, 'Your eyes are too pure to look on evil; you cannot tolerate wrong. Why then do you tolerate the treacherous? Why are you silent while the wicked swallow up those more righteous than themselves?' (Hab 1:13). God revealed to Habakkuk that again there was a wider perspective. Babylon in turn was going to come under God's judgement. Habakkuk had asked his question in the context of what he knew about God's character. He discovered that contrary to appearances, God's character had not changed, and he was not going to tolerate evil.

Although he had an answer, it was still hard for Habakkuk to reconcile himself to God's solution to the situation. Often, however, we have no answers or explanations. We are left in the dark with events which just do not make sense to us. So how do we carry on trusting that God is in control, and that he knows what he is doing when these things happen? We need to remember that we have finite minds, and can only go so far in our understanding of God and the ways that he works. Also we should not try to reduce God to our limited understanding. Dr James Dobson quotes Isaiah 55:8-9, "'For my thoughts are not your thoughts, neither are your ways my ways,' declares the Lord. 'As the heavens are higher than the earth, so are my ways higher than your ways and my thoughts than your thoughts.'" He writes of these verses, 'Clearly, the Scripture tells us that we lack the capacity to grasp God's infinite mind or the way he intervenes in our lives. How arrogant of us to think otherwise! Trying to analyze His omnipotence is like an amoeba attempting to comprehend the behaviour of man.'[5]

Taking this into account then we, like Habakkuk, need to view our questions in the light of what we do know about God. If we think of God's power, majesty, and greatness then can we really doubt that he knows what he is doing? After all the terrible things that happened to Job, God's response was not to explain himself, but to challenge Job to consider his power through nature. Job's response was one of humility, 'Surely I spoke of things I did not understand, things too wonderful for me to know' (Job 42:3). Faced with this revelation of God and an awareness of his own limitation Job replied, 'I am unworthy – how can I reply to you? I put my hand over my mouth' (Job 40:4). Job's questions were not answered, but he had a fresh perspective of God from which to view what had happened, and which brought him down to size.

Thinking of God's love, integrity, justice, and faithfulness can we doubt that his purposes are good? Habakkuk faced the situation in his time by remembering the faithfulness of God in the past, and believing this would continue in the future. He could even say, 'Though the fig-tree does not bud and there are no grapes on the vine, though the olive crop fails and the fields produce no food, though there are no sheep in the pen and no cattle in the stalls, yet I will rejoice in the Lord, I will be joyful in God my Saviour' (Hab 3:17-18). When things got as bad as they possibly could get, Habakkuk was still going to trust God's faithfulness. So much more has now been now revealed to us of God's love and faithfulness through the cross. What we do know of the attributes of God, gives us the right perspective from which to view those things which we do not understand.

Accepting that God is God and that we have finite minds, thinking of what we do know of God, and that his perspective is not the same as ours, where do we go from here? In his book Ian Coffey used John the Baptist as an example of someone struggling with doubt whilst in prison. He wrote, 'We can't always see the whole picture or make sense of circumstances that seem uncontrolled. Like John in his lonely prison cell, we can feel isolated and afraid. At such moments we have a clear choice. We can either exercise trust or give way to doubt. The first is the way of faith, and the other the route of unbelief.'[6]

In this life we will always have questions, and things that do not make sense, but these are opportunities for our faith to grow. This was the challenge from James Dobson's book for me. In his final comments James Dobson writes, 'Our message boils down to this very simple understanding: there is nothing the Lord wants of us more than the exercise of our faith. He will do nothing to undermine it, and we cannot please him without it. To define the term again, faith is believing that which has no absolute proof (Hebrews 11:1). It is hanging tough when the evidence would have us bail out. It is determining to trust him when he has not answered all the questions or even assured a pain-free passage.'[7] I realised that I had a choice of whether to trust God or not, and this choice had to be made without anything making more sense than it did at that moment. I made the decision to trust God in spite of my unanswered questions. This was another defining moment for me.

Having reached that point, I had one further experience with my 'why' questions. I came across a meditation that involved imagining a meeting with Jesus in a special place.[8] The meditation guided you through the experience and the conversation with Jesus. One of the questions that Jesus asked was whether I had a question that I would like to ask him. I certainly did! My 'why' questions about Rick's death immediately sprang to mind, but I found I could not ask them. Sitting there with an awareness of the presence of Jesus, I suddenly could not ask him. I think I knew that they were questions that he would not answer, but more than that I realised that they were not my questions to ask. They were Rick's questions. So I simply stayed silent and let the truth of this sink in. Later I was reminded of the time after the resurrection, in John 21, when Jesus told Peter what was going to happen to him, and then Peter wanted to know what would happen to John. Jesus' reply made it clear that that was nothing to do with Peter, 'If I want him to remain alive until I return, what is that to you? You must follow me' (John 21:22). I was very glad I had not asked!

Reading through my journal from the beginning, I have realised how far I have come in my journey of trying to find answers to my questions. It has been slow, and often triggered pain, anger, and grief. I have found some partial answers, and some different perspectives from which to view those which will remain unanswered. I have realised that my faith cannot depend on my ability to understand what God is doing. I was challenged by the thought that you either trust God, or you do not. You need to make a choice. This level of trust is what is needed to follow God through thick and thin. By choosing to trust God without answers I have reached a place of acceptance. That doesn't mean that I don't still have the sense of loss, and the pain and grief. I still long to see Rick again, but I've accepted what has happened. I have accepted it even though it does not make sense to me; I know it does to God. I would never have thought that it was possible to reach this point, but I have, and the realisation that I have brings its own sense of peace.

Chapter 12- A dot in the distance

Finally we came to the top of a hill, and there was the car. Lunch was in sight! The only trouble was the car was only a dot in the distance, and there was a steep descent to get to it over uneven ground. At first it felt as though the car wasn't getting any closer, but gradually as we picked our way down the hill it became less distant. Even this last part could not be hurried, and was hard work. As with the rest of the walk I could only go at my own pace.

Progress was slow as I picked my way through all the things God was showing me, and as I continued to seek him. I explored using silence, stillness, listening to God, and contemplative prayer. My lack of motivation and concentration were a hindrance to me in finding stillness, but at various times I felt God was encouraging me to continue this exploration. God also showed me that he wanted to deal with 'clutter' in my life, so processing with Veronica became less about bereavement and more about my relationship with God, and exploring other areas of my life. This was very draining, but although it often didn't feel like it at the time it was a positive way forward.

Quiet days and retreats were an important part of this process, as were the various books I was reading. On a retreat I felt God was giving me the reassurance that I still needed time to work on recovery, and that brokenness can be a good starting point from which he can produce lovely things. There were a couple of pictures that meant a lot to me, flowers blooming in the desert, and the formation of a pearl from the grit in an oyster. I also wrote this quote in my journal, 'If we think that ministry can only come out of strength, we may have to do a major rethink. Ministry can also come out of our own brokenness. This is not to say that we can minister out of our disappointment, frustration and anger. But we can serve out of our vulnerability. For in that place, we will be all the more dependent on God and sensitive to the other person.'[1] All this gave me hope.

Another area where progress was slow was in selling the house. Having put our house on the market in April 2018 we had some viewings, but no offers were forthcoming. This wasn't bothering me much through the summer. The weather was lovely and we took days out, doing some of our favourite walks for the last time. It was the Peak District at its best, and it made me wonder why I wanted to move. I had to remind myself that not many summers in the Peak District were that good! After seven months with nothing happening, we got to the point where our boiler needed its annual service. It was declared unsafe, so we decided to take the house off the market to replace it. We also made other improvements, including updating the bathroom and more decorating, so we were once again living amidst chaos. This also meant I had to adjust to spending another winter in the north. As someone who feels the cold, I had really been looking forward to being somewhere warmer by the time winter came. I hadn't expected it to take so long, so I had stopped helping at the children's group. I felt as though I was living in limbo, and I was unable to commit myself to anything as I didn't know how long I would be there for.

It was in October 2018 that I began to seriously consider writing a book from my journals. I had vaguely thought about it as something to do in the future. I even knew that the title would be 'Through Thick and Thin,' but had got no further than that. It wasn't until I let the idea slip in conversation with Veronica, and it was met with an enthusiastic response, that I started to think that maybe the time to begin this had come. She saw it as part of the journey I was on, and once again gave me a notebook to get started in! I felt both excited and daunted by the prospect. I had felt a bit stuck, and I'd prayed before going to see Veronica that God would show me a way forward. This was not an answer I had expected! However, it did appeal to me in that writing a book was a connection to Rick. It was something that he had suggested to me in the past, although I'm certain this was not the book he had in mind! He had obviously felt I was capable of writing one. I could see that even if I didn't do anything with it once it was finished, the actual process of writing it would be a positive thing for me to do.

I considered it for a while, and decided that I wouldn't know if I could do it unless I tried. I knew I needed space to read through my journals and to plan, so I booked a holiday cottage for a week on the edge of Sheffield. This was a very special time, as I committed the book to God and he strengthened me to cope with reading the journals, not an easy read. I made notes and tried to plan the structure. This was something that changed several times in the course of writing, but at least I had made a tentative start. My week in Sheffield was also a time that helped my confidence. I enjoyed having the space and managing on my own. I got myself to a church on Sunday, and I even went for walks without getting lost! A Quiet Day at a centre nearby was special, so too were the times I spent with God on my own.

On returning home I found, as with the walk, progress on the book could only be at my own pace. It triggered pain and grief, which could be overwhelming, and it brought up further things that I needed to process with Veronica. There were times when I couldn't cope with it at all, and others when I felt too tired, or had no motivation to write. At other times,

I found it an encouraging thing to do. It showed me how far I had come, how God had been with me through it all, and how he'd provided for me in so many different ways. For some reason I found it much easier to deal with it all away from home, so I had another week of space, this time in Wales, where progress was made at a faster rate. The weather was lovely and a mixture of writing, exploring the area, spending time with God, and working things through did me a lot of good.

I did not write the chapters in order. Some were much harder than others, and I avoided those I couldn't face until my processing brought me to a place where I could tackle them. One of these was the chapter about the first six weeks after Rick's death. As I've mentioned before, I relived this every anniversary and found it very painful, so I didn't know how I was going to cope with writing about it. This changed for me on the fourth anniversary of his death when I felt challenged to let these memories go. I'd also been challenged more than once to lay down the grief and to pick up life. I wrote in my journal on that day, 'I felt God was asking me to let go of the grip all the bad memories have on me. Also that I'm the one who is letting myself be defined as a bereaved mother and by my mourning and that I need to let go of that. I will always have a sense of loss, I will always grieve but I can't keep letting it control my life.' As I laid these memories down in prayer, I took up my life going forward and my positive memories of Rick. I put that future life into God's hands and affirmed my trust in him. It was a very positive step forward, and I felt very peaceful having done it.

The next day I read Psalm 30:11-12, 'You turned my wailing into dancing; you removed my sackcloth and clothed me with joy, that my heart may sing your praises and not be silent. Lord my God I will praise you for ever.' It reminded me of being told at Scargill that 'it must be so silent in my heart at the minute'. This was something I knew I needed God to change for me. I wasn't sure I was ready for dancing yet, or what it meant in practice. Veronica pictured it as being at a ceilidh where nobody knows the dance; the caller teaches a few steps at a time, and its gradually put together to form a dance. The caller knows what it should look like, but the dancers don't, so they need to listen to the caller. I found this a strong image, and a reassurance that God would teach me the dance a step at a time. It also brought home the importance of listening to God.

I would never have thought it was possible that I could reach this point. In fact even in the days leading up to the fourth anniversary I would not have thought it possible. I had been dreading the day as much as usual. It was God who brought me to the place where these changes could be made. I was still a bereaved mother, but that was no longer all that I was. I felt in a different place. It also meant that as I came to write about the first six weeks, it was no longer as painful as it might have been. I did get upset, but I no longer felt gripped by the memories, and I found that I could walk away and leave them, and my mind didn't dwell on them. If I began to become overwhelmed I could use a distraction and this worked, which was something I had been unable to do in the past.

We eventually put the house back on the market, but as the lack of progress continued I began to realise why I had been struggling to engage with the whole process. I had expected to move to Dorset to be near to Rick and Helen. I had expected to be able to talk to him about it all and for him to share in the process. As this could no longer happen, it felt as though everything else was second best, and I could not feel the same enthusiasm for it. Although it didn't solve anything, it helped me to recognise this, and to adapt and think about ways I could include Rick in the move. I realised that having things of his in the new house was going to be important to me. It meant that when we eventually received an offer, I was able to write in my journal that I knew I was ready for this to happen. God had been using the time in different ways to bring me to this point.

We started house hunting on line, and then went down to Sussex to view some properties. We were on the second day of this when the offer was withdrawn! I felt very confused by this, and it was very hard to go back to square one. Walking on the top of the Downs, I was expressing my frustration, and questioning God about what he was trying to show us. The words, 'Be still and know that I am God' (Ps 46:10) came strongly into my mind. I felt peaceful again about the move, and knew I'd got to keep trusting God for the way forward. Amazingly there was suddenly a lot more interest in our house, and we received another offer fairly soon after this. Another trip down to Sussex, and we found two houses we liked. We put in an offer on one of them, only for it then to be taken off the market! We decided it was too difficult trying to buy a house from a distance, so we carried on with the sale of our house. We completed in December 2019 and moved to Sussex leaving our furniture in storage. Having waited for so long it all happened in a matter of weeks at the end. At the same time Anna was also buying her first house. This was completed so that her things were moved out of our house with only two days to spare! It was a relief when it was all over.

The other house we had liked was not where we had been looking initially. It was in the town I had been brought up in, and was just round the corner from my mother. I had to adjust to this as I had wanted to be near my mother, but somewhere new. We put in an offer, which was accepted, and then spent the next three months in a holiday cottage. This was a positive time as I had space to continue with writing, and we did a lot of walking. We knew that a lot of things could go wrong with the purchase of a house, but we weren't expecting a pandemic to be one of them! We went into lockdown and no progress could be made. We moved in with my mother, and I realised that the timing was perfect as we were able to be with her during this lockdown. I continued writing, and, although hard, it was helpful to have something else to focus on during this difficult time, when everything felt uncertain and out of control. Having lost Rick to a virus I was very afraid of losing someone else I loved to Covid. As lockdown was eased we were able to continue with the purchase, which was proving not to be straightforward. We eventually completed two years, two months, and two days after we had first put our house on the market!

I had been uncertain about this house all the way through, but had gone along with it because once I'd adjusted to it, the location felt right. Although there had been problems along the way with the purchase, the door had never been shut on it, and there were very few properties coming onto the market, so I felt it was where God wanted us to be. However, that didn't stop me feeling very disappointed when I first walked into our new home that I had waited such a long time for. I had wanted our new house to need very little doing to it, but it certainly didn't fulfil that criteria! Nothing major, but we were constantly finding things that needed repairing, and it needed decorating throughout. Anna had been very encouraging and supportive through the purchasing process, and she particularly helped at this point. Surprisingly, I moved fairly quickly to feeling more positive, and to seeing it as a challenge and a chance to make it our own. We were very fortunate in that we didn't have to move in straight away. God provided for us again in that we managed to find people to come to do the work surprisingly quickly.

Especially helpful was the carpenter who could turn his hand to a lot of other things as well. Looking back I could see God's hand on the whole process, and I had been aware throughout that he was giving me the strength to deal with it all, and was keeping me remarkably calm.

I did miss Rick in all of this, and I longed to be able to talk to him about it all. Anna was doing a good job, but I wanted him to be part of it too. Veronica suggested that I should spend time on my own in the house and go into each room 'with' Rick. This was one of the times I felt I wanted to write to Rick, so I went into each room writing to him about things I thought he would have been interested in. This felt like a positive thing to have done, and it felt more as if I'd included him in the house. It helped even more when our furniture arrived and I had things of Rick's around me. These were things that connected me to him, and for that reason I treasured them, even the aforementioned rubbish bin! Memories of Rick were obviously with me too, and were something that I also treasured. I could think of them more easily, especially the happy ones, but they were, and always will be, accompanied by the pain of loss. Veronica had helped me to realise that some of the memories I have of Rick could still be of positive use to me. He was no longer here to encourage me, but I have the memory of his encouragement and that he believed in me, both of which can still have a positive impact on me. They are part of the legacy he has left me.

During this time Helen remarried, and I was so pleased for her. It was something I very much wanted for her, but that didn't mean that it didn't hurt. She and Dave were both very sensitive in their handling of the situation, and in reassuring me that my initial fears of losing Helen were unfounded. Helen had spent three years doing an MA, and we were very proud of her achieving this, given all she had been going through. Dave had her MA certificate framed with the words 'For Rick' on the bottom of the frame. I was very moved by this and so grateful for his attitude towards Rick. I was also touched by the fact that Helen wanted to keep Rick's surname to form a double-barrelled name with Dave's. I was even more touched that Dave changed his to be the same. I felt she had found someone special in that he was willing to respect Rick's memory in these ways.

Anna has now settled into her new home. She is no longer receiving support and we are proud of the way she is managing life with her illness. Being such a distance from her during lockdown has been hard for us all, but she has coped really well. She works at a dog rescue centre and fosters dogs. She has proved to be very good at handling nervous and difficult dogs.

Over half of this book has been written since I have been in Sussex. Writing it has definitely been part of the healing process for me. It has also been a connection to Rick, which I have valued. I had always had a little niggle at the back of my mind as I read words of encouragement, and things that gave me hope. I would question whether these things would actually happen for me. They often seemed so far ahead of the place I was actually in, and I wondered whether I would be the exception that proved the rule. Writing this book has made me aware of the truth of the things I took hope from. Nobody's journey is the same, but a thread of hope that such a journey is possible runs through them all.

Looking back has given me a fresh perspective on this time and the process I was going through. As its name suggests, a journey through thick and thin is hard work. Grieving is hard work. At first, just getting through each day was hard work. Coping with the continuous stream of difficult circumstance that came our way was hard work. Working through what my faith meant to me, and how to cope with the unanswered questions was hard work. Doing the scrap book, reading books, my times with Veronica, and writing were all hard work. It's no wonder I often felt exhausted and overwhelmed. I can see now that I was often too hard on myself. I felt I should be doing better, but there is no time schedule for grief. Even towards the end of the walk, where the end was in sight, it had made no difference to the pace at which I could go. In the same way grieving had to continue at my own pace, it could not be hurried.

As I wonder how I did actually manage to survive this devastating and truly terrible time, it has opened my eyes more fully to just how much God has done for me. I cannot stress enough that this journey of following God through thick and thin, was certainly not something I did in my own strength. It could definitely only be undertaken in God's strength. Sometimes I followed where God was leading, at other times I shut him out, and at others the effort of communicating with him simply seemed too much. Nevertheless, God has helped me, provided for me, taught me, and continually reached out to me. He has encouraged me, reassured me, and challenged me. He has brought me healing and hope. I have learnt afresh to trust him. I think my journey has far more to do with God's faithfulness to me through thick and thin, rather than the other way round, but nonetheless the journey so far has been made.

Starting a new life here in Sussex has been put on hold due to the pandemic, and I have no idea what that life might look like in the future. This is certainly not the fresh start I was envisaging! Once again it all feels out of control, but God has brought me this far and I can only trust that he will continue to strengthen and guide me in the future. One thing

I do know is that grieving, loss, and pain will always be part of that future. There are so many things for me now, which are bittersweet. I still experience grief triggers, and feel the pain of loss. There are still times when I struggle, especially around the tree stump days. The concept of continuing bonds and finding links with Rick is still a positive thing for me, but I miss Rick very much, and always will. I have found this statement by Gary Roe to be true, 'As we grieve, our children get assimilated into our lives in new ways. We don't move on without them or leave them behind. They become even more a part of us. We heal, but we're not the same. We learn to live with a hole in our hearts.' He goes on to say, 'On some level, we will never stop grieving. We will always miss them. We will never forget.'[2]

The hardest walk I have ever done ended when I reached the car, which is where the comparison ends. Unlike the walk, my journey of following God through thick and thin continues.

Now to him who is able to do immeasurably
more than all we ask or imagine,
according to his power that is at work within us,
to him be glory in the church and in Christ Jesus
throughout all generations, for ever and ever! Amen.

Ephesians 3:20-21

Notes

Chapter 5

1. Jean Watson, *Bereavement* (The Bible Reading Fellowship 2005).
2. Ibid., p. 10.
3. Ibid., p. 25.
4. Ibid., p. 16.
5. Ian Coffey, *Postcards from the Edge: Finding God in Hard Places* (Inter-Varsity Press 2015), p. 24.
6. Ibid., p. 25.
7. Ibid., p. 40.

Chapter 6

1. *Quiet Spaces* January – April 2016 (The Bible Reading Fellowship 2016), pp. 44-45.
2. Ibid., pp. 68-69, 71.
3. Ibid., pp. 9-10.

Chapter 8

1. Sarah Young, *Jesus Calling* (Thomas Nelson 2004)
2. Ann Voskamp, *You have enough of Me* (www.facebook.com/AnnVoskamp/photos)
3. 'Broken Pieces' is included in a series of poetry books written by Helen Brocklehurst, and published and sold by Scargill to raise money for various causes. Copies are available by contacting admin@scargillmovement.org

Chapter 9

1. Philippa Skinner, *See you soon* (Presence Books in partnership with Spoonbill Publications 2012), p. xvi
2. Ibid., p. 108
3. The Northumbria Community, *Celtic Daily Prayer Book Two: Farther Up and Farther In* (William Collins 2015), p. 867

Chapter 10

1. Gary Roe, *Shattered: Surviving the Loss of a Child* (Healing Resources Publishing 2017), p. 125
2. Ibid., p. 125
3. Ibid., p. 184
4. Ibid., pp. 184-185

Chapter 11

1. Gary Roe, *Shattered: Surviving the Loss of a Child* (Healing Resources Publishing 2017), p. 108
2. Dr James Dobson, *When God Doesn't Make Sense* (Tyndale House Publishers, Inc.), p. 13
3. John Stott, *Through The Bible Through The Year* (Monarch Books 2006), p. 267
4. As well as Dr James Dobson's book *When God Doesn't Make Sense* there were two other books I found particularly helpful whilst reflecting on this issue. The first was a series of Bible readings given at Keswick by Jonathan Lamb on Habakkuk published in *Out of Control?* (Authentic Media 2004), pp. 5-69. The second was R. T. Kendall, *Totally Forgiving God* (Hodder & Stoughton 2012).

5. Dr James Dobson, *When God Doesn't Make Sense* (Tyndale House Publishers, Inc.), p. 8
6. Ian Coffey, *Postcards from the Edge: Finding God in Hard Places* (Inter-Varsity Press 2015), p. 80
7. Dr James Dobson, *When God Doesn't Make Sense* (Tyndale House Publishers, Inc.), p. 221
8. *Quiet Spaces* May – August 2016 (The Bible Reading Fellowship 2016), pp. 17-19

Chapter 12
1. The Northumbria Community, *Celtic Daily Prayer Book Two: Farther Up and Farther In* (William Collins 2015), p. 1319
2. Gary Roe, *Shattered: Surviving the Loss of a Child* (Healing Resources Publishing 2017), p. 209